ARCHITECTURAL DESIGN

GUEST-EDITED BY
CHARLES JENCKS
AND FAT

RADICAL POST-MODERNISM

05|2011

ARCHITECTURAL DESIGN
VOL 81, NO 5
SEPTEMBER/OCTOBER 2011
ISSN 0003-8504

PROFILE NO 213
ISBN 978-0470-669884

wiley.com

GUEST-EDITED BY
CHARLES JENCKS
AND FAT

RADICAL POST-MODERNISM

*Jencks and Koolhaas exchange on
Post–Modernism, preservation, the
evil aura of the word 'iconic' and
the Big Mac sandwich diagram.*

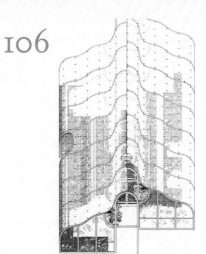

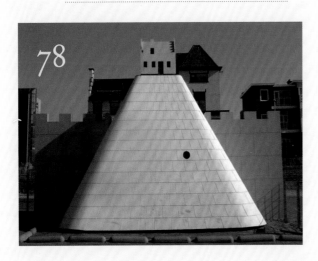

*The 1980 Venice Architecture Biennale
brought Post-Modernism to the world's
attention, but also highlighted the tensions
between historicism and communication.*

ARCHITECTURAL DESIGN
SEPTEMBER/OCTOBER 2011
PROFILE NO 213

Editorial Offices
John Wiley & Sons
25 John Street
London
WC1N 2BS

T: +44 (0)20 8326 3800

Editor
Helen Castle

Managing Editor (Freelance)
Caroline Ellerby

Production Editor
Elizabeth Gongde

Design and Prepress
Artmedia, London

Art Direction and Design
CHK Design:
Christian Küsters
Hannah Dumphy

Printed in Italy by Conti Tipocolor

Sponsorship/advertising
Faith Pidduck/Wayne Frost
T: +44 (0)1243 770254
E: fpidduck@wiley.co.uk

Subscribe to AD

AD is published bimonthly and is
available to purchase on both a
subscription basis and as individual
volumes at the following prices.

Prices
Individual copies: £22.99 / US$45
Mailing fees may apply

Annual Subscription Rates
Student: £75 / US$117 print only
Individual: £120 / US$189 print only
Institutional: £200 / US$375
print or online
Institutional: £230 / US$431 combined
print and online

Subscription Offices UK
John Wiley & Sons Ltd
Journals Administration Department
1 Oldlands Way, Bognor Regis
West Sussex, PO22 9SA
T: +44 (0)1243 843272
F: +44 (0)1243 843232
E: cs-journals@wiley.co.uk

Print ISSN: 0003-8504;
Online ISSN: 1554-2769

Prices are for six issues and include
postage and handling charges.
Individual rate subscriptions must be
paid by personal cheque or credit card.
Individual rate subscriptions may not
be resold or used as library copies.

All prices are subject to change
without notice.

Rights and Permissions
Requests to the Publisher should
be addressed to:
Permissions Department
John Wiley & Sons Ltd
The Atrium
Southern Gate
Chichester
West Sussex PO19 8SQ
England

F: +44 (0)1243 770620
E: permreq@wiley.co.uk

Front cover: FAT, The Villa, Hoogvliet, The
Netherlands, 2008 © Maarten Laupman
Inside front cover: Concept CHK Design

EDITORIAL
Helen Castle

Post-Modernism is simultaneously the most controversial and fascinating architectural movement of recent decades. Never has a style been by turns so all pervasive and then so abruptly unfashionable. Embraced in the late 1970s and 1980s by designers and clients alike, by the early 1990s it had come to be regarded by the architectural community as synonymous with the worst of commercial architecture and classical pastiche. The very word 'Post-Modern' is still likely to evoke knee-jerk revulsion in the majority of architects over 40.

The prospect of the V&A's retrospective exhibition 'Postmodernism: Style and Subversion 1970–1990' afforded 𝐃 a wonderful excuse to re-examine Post-Modern architecture. Rather than revisit the Post-Modern movement in its entirety, something that Charles Jencks has done in his definitive and highly readable new book on the subject, *The Story of Post-Modernism: Five Decades of the Ironic, Iconic and Critical in Architecture*, the aim of this issue of 𝐃 is to look at contemporary architectural culture. This led to an unlikely but highly creative partnership between Charles Jencks and Sean Griffiths, Charles Holland and Sam Jacob of FAT. Whereas Jencks played a defining role as the original voice and disseminator of the Post-Modern with his best-selling book of 1977, *The Language of Post-Modern Architecture*, FAT realised the potency of Post-Modern ideas for contemporary architecture during the movement's darkest hour in the mid-1990s. As they state in their introduction: "There was something both immediately compelling and highly provocative in Post-Modernism's toxic un-fashionability."

If I played the part of matchmaker between Jencks and FAT, the formulation of Radical Post-Modernism (RPM) was entirely a product of their collaboration. The prefix 'Radical' clearly demarcates this current tendency from the corporate ersatz of the late 1980s, but it is more than this. It is a reminder of Post-Modernism's more serious intentions in the late 1960s, as encapsulated by the work of early protagonists such as Robert Venturi. In his introduction, Jencks accordingly identifies three core concepts of Radical Post-Modernism: communication, formal tropes and social content. For FAT and other architects of their generation, Post-Modernism also offers the opportunity to provide "a wider sense of belonging to a Post-Modernist culture that encompasses film, literature, philosophy, sciences and a host of other disciplines". Importantly for them as a practice, it also offers them a means by which to deal with architecture's relationship with fashion and taste, particularly that of the everyday, as suggested by their acronym FAT (Fashion Architecture Taste). 𝐃

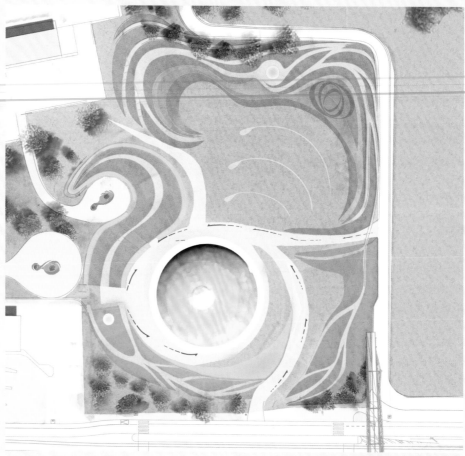

Charles Jencks, Plan for Green Oasis at CERN (European Organization for Nuclear Research), Geneva, 2011
top: The Green Oasis is designed to become the central area of CERN's Globe structure, the heart of the growing complex. The landforms protect and set off the Globe, while their circular layout and iconography are based on the symbolic programme of the Cosmic Ring. This depicts the smallest things in the universe to the biggest, and the circular layout also reflects the 27-kilometre (10.42-mile) accelerator.

FAT, Community in a Cube (CIAC), Middlesbrough, 2011
above: View from the south showing the garden courtyard and the 'Sky Home' apartments which take the form of pitched-roofed suburban houses that sit on top of an otherwise typical Modernist apartment block.

Charles Jencks

Sean Griffiths

Charles Holland

Sam Jacob

This issue of ∆ has been co-edited by Charles Jencks with Sean Griffiths, Charles Holland and Sam Jacob of Fashion Architecture Taste (FAT). FAT's work has helped to instigate a critical reappraisal of Post-Modernism, an architectural category defined by Charles Jencks in his 1977 book *The Language of Post-Modern Architecture*.

Charles Jencks is an American architectural theorist, author and landscape architect. He has written widely on Post-Modern and Modern architecture. His bestselling book, *The Language of Post-Modern Architecture* (Academy, 1977), popularised Post-Modernism in architecture and established him as the international authority on the subject. His most recent book, *The Story of Post-Modernism: Five Decades of Ironic, Iconic and Critical Architecture* (John Wiley & Sons, 2011), provides a definitive overview of the movement from the 1960s to the present. Jencks is also an influential landscape architect: in 2004 his landform for the Scottish National Gallery of Modern Art, Edinburgh, won the Gulbenkian Prize for Museums; he is currently undertaking projects in Europe, including an iconographic and green project for CERN (the European Organization for Nuclear Research) in Geneva. His celebrated garden in Scotland is the subject of his book *The Garden of Cosmic Speculation* (Frances Lincoln, 2003), while his recent landscape work is summarised in *The Universe in the Landscape* (Frances Lincoln, 2011). In the late 1990s, Jencks established the Maggie Centres with his late wife Maggie Keswick, a charity that has become influential in providing uplifting, caring environments for cancer patients, designed by some of the world's most cutting-edge architects. He continues to lecture internationally on architecture and landscape design.

FAT is an architectural practice run by Sean Griffiths, Charles Holland and Sam Jacob. Their work is characterised by an interest in the politics of taste and space, and the role of communication in architecture. Established in 1995, the practice's work has evolved from urban-based art projects through the scales of design, interiors and architecture to masterplans. Their award-winning work receives international attention and has been exhibited and published extensively. Current projects include a new studio complex for the BBC in Cardiff and a residential scheme in Middlesbrough. Griffiths, Holland and Jacob are visiting professors at Yale University School of Architecture, teach at institutions including the Architectural Association (AA) and the University of Westminster in London, and are regular contributors to magazines and journals. A shared interest in the legacy and potential contemporary relevance of architectural Post-Modernism has led FAT and Charles Jencks to jointly co-edit this issue of ∆.

SPOTLIGHT

Atelier Bow-Wow

Double Chimney, Karuizawa, Nagano, Japan, 2008
An archetypal house is split and folded open to create an architecture that is somehow both familiar and radically altered.

Today's Radical Post-Modernists are magpie-like in their use of references, forms and decoration. Highly creative, they innovatively employ ornamentation, supergraphics, collage and iconography: values or qualities that are all classified by FAT in their Post-Modern matrix on p 47. In a highly knowing culture, formal exuberance has become just as much of a design strategy as the pared back.

The Villa, Hoogvliet, The Netherlands, 2008
The external surface of the Villa acts as a
supergraphic wrapped around a generic
industrial structure. The graphics narrative
gathers specific contextual references that
are then projected as a speculative idea
of contemporary civicness for the satellite
new town of Hoogvliet.

Forum La Caixa, Madrid, 2008
Herzog & de Meuron takes existing urban
fragments and makes a holistic collage from
them in the vertical dimension. The bottom
of the city is opened up to movement, the
old brick facades are lifted off the ground to
hold the museum, and the top floor imitates
in shape and ornament the morphology and
style of Madrid's past culture, including the
Arabic. Thus preservation is mixed with
paraphrasing, repair and rewriting. Like the
reminted coins of Rome, these palimpsests
make an enjoyable art of urban time.

Images: pp 8-9 Atelier Bow-Wow; p 10 © Maarten Laupman; p 11 © Charles Jencks; p 12 © FAT; p 13 © John Gollings

← **FAT**

↓ **ARM**

**'You Make Me Feel Mighty Real',
Northumberland, 2000**
A miniature Romanesque church forms a
shimmering place of contemplation within
the apparently natural, but actually manmade
landscape of Belsay Hall.

National Museum of Australia, Canberra, 2001
The museum plan collides a number of 'as-
found' objects, most notably Libeskind's Jewish
Museum, Charles Moore's Piazza d'Italia and
Frank Gehry's flamboyant fish-shaped forms.

WHAT IS RADICAL POST-MODERNISM?

The iconic building during the credit crunch, *pace* the discontents, is growing not slowing. Witness in London the return of the Pinnacle, the Shard, the Walkie Talkie and, of course, the Cheesegrater. These skyscrapers may be commercial metaphors, very late capitalist and very overbearing, but they do seek to communicate their dumb metaphors as iconic buildings. So PoMo is back too, not just the more nourishing RPM.

FOA, Ravensbourne, London, 2010
opposite top: All-over ornament based on an aperiodic tiling
pattern in three basic colours. Post-Modern architects look to
nature and the cosmos for instruction, and here the quasi-crystal
and fractal growth are invoked. Note the superordinate patterns
that emerge: the diagonals, circles of varying size and target
shapes – a symphonic order that delights as it edifies.

Herzog & de Meuron, Forum La Caixa, Madrid, 2008
opposite bottom: The Time City made explicit as the industrial
brick warehouse is partly saved, lifted above the street to connect
two squares, and the top floors given a morphology in rusted iron
that relates to those on all sides: contextual counterpoint.

Since the millennium, Post-Modernism in architecture
has returned with a vengeance in all but name. After the
transitional 1990s, when Neo-Modernism became the default
style of choice, this plural tradition flowered again with the
iconic building and ornamental patterns in architecture.
Ironically this blossoming of the PoMo agenda was greatly
helped by the disappearance of the term. Most everyone was
sick of the moniker, and some epigones of the movement,
such as Robert Venturi, even denied publicly that they were
members of this club (that would have them).[1]

It became an un-fashion in architecture for the same
reason that Modernism had expired: commercial success,
followed by debasement. Post-Modern architecture started to
go through this unfortunate thinning out in the mid-1980s,
when Philip Johnson and the Disney Corporation 'gave it the
kiss' (as I wrote in later editions of *The Language of Post-
Modern Architecture*,[2] and as Kester Rattenbury describes
on pp 106–13 of this issue). At first, critical of the ruling
mode of orthodox Modernism, it too became clichéd when
it became a reigning mode of late capitalism. Commerce,
success, the establishment once again claimed a living
culture, as happened with its parent. Thus its terminological
death was necessary before some of its better work could be
constructed – post the year 2000 – by Herzog & de Meuron,
Peter Zumthor and Peter Eisenman among many others. In
effect, the agenda was reborn minus the name, a condition
debated by Rem Koolhaas and me on pp 32–45.

When Helen Castle asked FAT and me to edit this issue
of *D* on Post-Modernism, we looked for another term to
distinguish what was important about the agenda, and
unsurprisingly came up with the old 1960s prefix 'radical'.
Three core concepts underlie our usage of the phrase.

Communication, and its attendant qualities – metaphor,
iconography, symbolism, image, surface, narrative, irony –
was one value that ties together the 1960s concerns and
those of today. It constitutes the first part of our common
definition of Radical Post-Modernism (RPM). Robert Venturi,
Minoru Takeyama, James Stirling or, today, Koolhaas,
Herzog & de Meuron and Frank Gehry all seek an expressive
architecture that communicates to a broad audience, one
that plays the high game of Lutyens and the low game of
Main Street, one that uses irony to send a double message

to a double audience, and iconic metaphors to stimulate
the public. The iconic building during the credit crunch,
pace the discontents, is growing not slowing. Witness in
London the return of the Pinnacle, the Shard, the Walkie
Talkie and, of course, the Cheesegrater. These skyscrapers
may be commercial metaphors, very late capitalist and very
overbearing, but they do seek to communicate their dumb
metaphors as iconic buildings. So PoMo is back too, not just
the more nourishing RPM.

The *formal tropes* of today's Post-Modernism obviously
grew out of yesterday: complexity and contradiction, ornament
and multiple articulation, collage and juxtaposition, layering
and ambiguity, multivalence and double coding. For Foreign
Office Architects (FOA) and Cecil Balmond, as so many other
digital designers, ornament has returned as an adjunct of
pattern making, of form and material considered at a smaller
scale than structure and skin. Of course Modernists made
structure and construction into a repressed ornament, which
they could not admit because of the Loosian taboo, so what
is different about this return is that it is full blown, admitted.
They wrap their whole building with exuberant 'affect', as
they call it. Even Minimalists such as Zumthor exaggerate
materiality and burn out their wooden interiors to great
empathetic effect. So many recognisable, and smell-able,
tropes unite these RPMs.

Social content is the third concern that underlies our
common definition of radical, framed in several ways. It refers
to relating buildings to their context not just fitting in, but what
I have called 'contextual counterpoint' (see pp 62–67); that is,
transforming adjacent themes in striking ways. Social content
for FAT refers to activism, process, working for working-class
housing, and for me as well the 'pluralism of taste'. The social
agenda seeks to appeal to different classes and ethnic groups.
If an RPM building does not satisfy every taste, then at least it
seeks to reach the users, as well as to stimulate the passer-
by. That is, it addresses a complex and contradictory task,
seeks to provoke a sensual and haptic reaction, and make
people feel an architectural presence. Contrary to professional
wisdom, the ugly, the rebarbative and the cheapskate (to use
Gehry's coinage) can all play a role as part of the aesthetic.
Indeed, repellent qualities are themselves aesthetic and work
effectively in contrast with elegance (as every artist knows)

FAT, Islington Square, New Islington, Manchester, 2006
below: Supergraphics in coloured brick change the scale and meaning of this working-class housing and take the deprivation out of mass housing at £1,000 per square metre. Like Ralph Erskine at the Byker Wall 30 years previously, this Post-Modernism was born in consultation with the inhabitants, the 23 individual clients given various choices, and like 19th-century spec-built it is 'Queen Anne in front and Mary Anne behind', an appropriate contrast of public and private space.

David Chipperfield, Neues Museum, Berlin, 2009
bottom: Various strategies – repair, restoration, conservation and paraphrase – were used here to pull together a ruin, creating another Time City of fragments in beautiful tension.

As Anthony Blunt argued in 'Some Uses and Abuses of the Terms Baroque and Rococo in Architecture',[3] there are no perfectly and completely Baroque and Rococo buildings because the category is always more capacious and contradictory than any single structure. So it is with RPM.

as long as they are wrapped into the larger narrative and tastes. Here the 19th-century arguments for character rather than exclusive beauty are important. For instance, the work of FAT takes Venturi's oppositions between the beautiful and ugly, expensive and cheap, to new contradictory levels, and this is relevant to the social agenda. It is not Bucky Fuller's 'Madame, how much does your house weigh?' (a sexist slight), but 'Sir, why should your backside be as luxurious as your front?' (a question of resources and acknowledging social reality). Ethically and aesthetically these dualities are more relevant than the all-over aesthetic, what has become today the 'seamless artifice' of other tastes, the Neo-Modernists, classicists and some 'digiterati'. For the large buildings of a complex society, an integrated taste leaves a bad taste. Total integration is fine for a pavilion.

The matrix on page 47 of this issue shows the 12 values of RPM and as applied to its practitioners. However, in putting together this list we became aware of two welcome facts: no architect or building is completely RPM. Either reality would be overbearing. Beyond that the variety of definers brings out a historical point. As Anthony Blunt argued in 'Some Uses and Abuses of the Terms Baroque and Rococo in Architecture',[3] there are no perfectly and completely Baroque and Rococo buildings because the category is always more capacious and contradictory than any single structure. So it is with RPM. Nonetheless, there are recent exemplars which help define the idea.

Consider Modernists who occasionally stray into this territory. Norman Foster designs highly communicative icons today in important historical contexts, the multiple metaphors for Swiss Re in London (2004) or the Sage music centre in Gateshead (2004), or such one-liners as the Sheikh al Zayed National Museum in Abu Dhabi (2010–), based on falcon wing tips. His Reichstag in Berlin (1999) refers obliquely to the historical dome, 1920s Expressionism and contemporary DNA, and he has redesigned old symbols such as the double-headed eagle. More significantly, by preserving graffiti of the occupying Russians he has accepted multiple tastes. A similar momentary shift is evident in David Chipperfield's Neues Museum in Berlin (2009), a reworking of the past, present and future in an ad-hoc way. Here different periods and events are melded together, they are whitewashed, unified

and separated with some style. Both Modernists may have been urged towards pluralism by their clients and the public, but their Berlin buildings are still examples of RPM. And this occasional (and client induced) practice points to another conclusion: RPM is a genre to be picked up and used where appropriate, and not a panacea for every building. Ubiquitous RPM would be as grotesque as any style applied universally.

When Post-Modernism was defined in the other arts, sciences and cultural forms, it was understood as 'subversion from within' the establishment, using the reigning voice to send a different message. In architecture irony continues to play this role, but here we have included a look at the street art of Banksy (see pp 114–21) because it so clearly raises issues of subverting customary codes – those of lawyers, professional artists and the art market. The social content of his work attacks political repression in Palestine, the mad overvaluing of Jeff Koons and others, as well as the authenticity of street art (graffiti) itself. All is artfully put in question by this wit and double coding, a potential inspiration for RPM architecture.

If communication is of fundamental concern to RPM, then we have returned to 'The Presence of the Past', the title of the 1980 Venice Biennale, the first international exhibition of architecture that sought to reach a large public and did so with a rich language (see pp 98–105). Here was a fateful moment when Post-Modernism was pulled towards historicism, but kept its commitment to a plural language and plural audience. Some damned it from this moment on as nothing but signs stuck on sheds, but its more radical origins survived this detour. Post-Modernism was the only 'ism' besides its parent to last for many years, and not become a 'wasm', and permeate all areas of culture. Its stealth emergence in architecture since the year 2000 gives a new take on the old cliché: sometimes history repeats itself better if the architects don't know it. In 50 years Post-Modernism has one partial victory to its credit in opening up the legitimacy of many traditions; ask the modern classicists or Deconstructivists or community architects if you doubt this. The historian John Summerson said its original claim was to insist that 'Modernism could die' when he, like most people, thought it was immortal, and therefore inevitable.[4] Market pluralism is not the same as political and cultural pluralism, and PoMo has much to do in its unfinished project.

POST-MODERNISM
AN INCOMPLETE PROJECT

By FAT

The artist Dan Graham once said that the most radical thing to do at any given time was that which was most recently fashionable.[5] Such things are the least value to capitalism, when the time lag between their rejection and subsequent reappropriation is the longest. This is the moment when the sheen of desire fades and the dynamics of commodification are laid bare. Beyond this, their reintroduction disrupts the apparently seamless phantasmagoria of late-capitalist cultures.

This is how Post-Modernism appeared to us in the mid-1990s. It had gone from the style of architecture most likely to win you planning permission for a new office block in the City of London, to the least. It had vanished from the pages of fashionable magazines and from the drawing boards of architects and students, a skeleton in the plan chest. In its wake came a return to Modernism shorn of its social and political convictions. The Hi Tech school of Norman Foster, Richard Rogers and Nicholas Grimshaw dominated large public commissions, while obsessively tasteful Minimalism was *de rigueur* in retail and domestic architecture.

There was something both immediately compelling and highly provocative in Post-Modernism's toxic unfashionability. In embracing and recycling the detritus of capitalism – reclaiming a style that was once the emblem of corporatism – we could confront a number of architectural taboos. Chief among these was the issue of fashion itself. Post-Modernism implicitly acknowledged the fact that architecture, as a product of capitalism, was itself subject to fashion, a category that according to the puritanically righteous represents all that is facile, superfluous and superficial.

Rather than acknowledging the conditions of late-capitalist culture, perhaps most succinctly described by the geographer David Harvey as a 'time/space'[6] compression which leads to unending and often disorienting change, architects prefer to cling to a myth of timelessness. In doing so they fail to acknowledge that architecture's attempts to achieve authenticity are as subject to fashion, and therefore as open to appropriation by capitalism, as the length of a skirt at any given moment.

For the record, since the 'death' of architectural Post-Modernism in the late 1980s, architecture has been subject to a number of fleeting fashions, including Neo-Modernism, Deconstructivism, Minimalism, iconicism and parametricism. What these fashion cycles reveal is that Post-Modernism as an architectural style may have died, but post-modernism as a pervasive cultural condition certainly has not. In fact, it has only accelerated along with globalisation and the neo-liberal free market economy.

Architecture's recent obsessions with the icon and the iconographic symbol are only the most overt manifestations of a continuing relevance of Post-Modernism. Explicit surface decoration, ornamentation and the return of the figurative are also strong seams in contemporary architecture. An interest in computer-generated decoration has led to the 'digital Baroque' style of architects like Gage Clemenceau or Evan Douglis, practices that use Modernist techniques to create decidedly un-Modernist forms. But this is not the reason for writing this issue of Δ. There is something else, something that explains the radical part of the equation. Why is Post-Modernism radical? How can a style co-opted by the Disney Corporation as 'entertainment architecture' and that has continued in various modes since the 1980s possibly claim to be radical today?

Whatever Happened to (Post) Modernism?

In *Whatever Happened to Modernism?*[7] Gabriel Josipovici argues that the essential characteristics of Modernism can be limited to neither abstraction nor technological innovation and indeed, that the kind of abstraction promoted by the likes of Abstract Expressionist high priest Clement Greenberg did not represent the essence of Modernism at all, but acted merely as a sign for it. Josipovici, interestingly, suggests that the key characteristic of Modernism is recognition of a loss of authority after the Reformation, resulting from the demise of a religious culture which was widely shared and which had conferred authority because it claimed to be universal.

Following this logic, he claims that *Don Quixote* was a Modernist work because of the polyphonic, circumspect and

Architecture's recent obsessions
with the icon and the iconographic
symbol are only the most overt
manifestations of a continuing
relevance of Post-Modernism.

Here, other external voices represented by the found text in the newspaper fragments also avoid the central voice of authority. These are precisely the same issues and tactics that Post-Modernism pursued: those of multiple authorship, multivalence, collage, quotation and a decentred authority.

deliberately uncertain character of its writing. This formative
example of the novel used a gaggle of different storytellers
relating fragments of the story in order to avoid the sense of an
authorial authority. Similarly, Josipovici notes Picasso's use of
newspaper collage in 1912 as another means of creating a
system of quotation. Here, other external voices represented by
the found text in the newspaper fragments also avoid the central
voice of authority. These are precisely the same issues and tactics
that Post-Modernism pursued: those of multiple authorship,
multivalence, collage, quotation and a decentred authority.

Josipovici is writing about literature and art and, of
course, Post-Modernism in these subjects is considerably less
contentious than it is in architecture. In fact at the same time
that they were rejecting their own version of Post-Modernism,
architects were happily embracing Post-Modernism in other
disciplines via the philosophy of Jean-François Lyotard and
Fredric Jameson and the cultural geography of David Harvey
and Edward Soja.

All the practitioners featured in this issue have no
doubt encountered these or other Post-Modern theorists.
This is perhaps why they are less self-conscious about
the charge of being labelled Post-Modern than were the
generation immediately before them. Perhaps, unlike previous
generations, they recognise that they are Post-Modernists in
a wider sense of belonging to a Post-Modernist culture that
encompasses film, literature, philosophy, sciences and a host
of other disciplines. It is this very awareness that makes them
radical. They implicitly reject the platitudes of an architectural
culture happy pursuing a hollowed-out, tastefully rendered
version of Modernism. This is evident in an explicit but critical
return to using ornamentation and historical decoration in
the work of architects like Hild und K and Caruso St John, as
well as the use of the kind of narrative and figurative elements
that appear in buildings by Atelier Bow-Wow and Edouard
François. Perhaps most tellingly of all is the rejection of the
idea of heroic originality and a consequent interest in reusing
and remaking familiar, everyday and sometimes wilfully
unoriginal elements.

They also recognise that there is no central narrative and
hence there must be many voices. They know that for those
voices to be able to tell their stories, there must be figuration,
ornament, narrative and communication. They know that the
formal tropes required to articulate these voices – collage,
juxtaposition, superimposition, quotation, parody – are those
developed in the early years of the 20th century, and in
recognising this they know that they – and not those who
cling to the hollow abstractions denuded of their social,
political and aesthetic meaning – are the true heirs to the
radicalism of early Modernism.

Post-Modernism is not, then, the disavowal of Modernism.
It is the continuation of it under different conditions and
armed with new weapons. So, this is not a revival and
revivalism is not our aim. Nevertheless, to celebrate Post-
Modernism today is a strange thing. As Reinhold Martin
suggests, to think of it as 'anything other than a lapsed
historical phenomenon or as a fait accompli may seem
quaintly anachronistic or even parochial'.[8] It remains a
moment that seems to resist reabsorption into contemporary
architectural culture. Perhaps, more likely given the way it
evokes reactions of distrust and even disgust (still), it is more
likely that this separation is a form of exile.

Radical Post-Modernism

Post-Modernism remains problematic precisely because it
poses difficult, vital questions for architecture that have never
gone away. This issue of *D* offers the chance to reconnect
with a radical strain of thought that began with Robert Venturi
and Denise Scott Brown's interest in the complexities of the
ordinary, that took in the micropolitics of taste and addressed
the dichotomies of high and low culture. It is also a joint
project between FAT and Charles Jencks, architectural Post-
Modernism's original definer and chronicler. It is therefore
a mix of voices itself: part historical overview, part survey
of current architectural versions of Post-Modernism and
part polemic. Hence also two introductions: aligned and
complementary but different.

If you were to imagine this issue of Δ as a road trip, we could think of the role the rear-view mirror plays: a glance backwards is part of the way we go forward.

The issue concludes with a top ten of Post-Modernism, an inventory of key moments in its evolution that includes work by James Stirling, Richard Hamilton, Hans Hollein, Charles Moore and others. It is our contention that the work initiated by these diverse architects and artists was part of a vital project to retune Modernism to the particularities of our age. Far from being a vacuous symbol of commercial greed, Post-Modernism offers us the possibility of critically engaging with the realities of the contemporary life.

If you were to imagine this issue of Δ as a road trip, we could think of the role the rear-view mirror plays: a glance backwards is part of the way we go forward. The strategies of Post-Modernism – artificially cauterised by the puritanical wing of architecture and dismissed as part of the unfashionable excesses of the 1980s – are a rich seam still to be mined. Post-Modernism, in that sense, remains an incomplete project.

Outline of the Issue

The issue is split, loosely, into three sections. The first explores the current cultural landscape and defines Radical Post-Modernist tendencies within it. Charles Jencks discusses this terrain with Rem Koolhaas, in relation to OMA's own work (see pp 32–45). Sam Jacob's essay 'Beyond the Flatline' (pp 24–31) examines the increasingly abstract landscape of digital culture, its ability to collapse space and time. What does this mean for Post-Modernism's binary opposition of high and low culture?

We have also curated a group of co-conspirators, some willing, some unwilling and some highly unlikely. Here we see a range of conceptions of architecture whose range spreads from activism to corporatism, but all working within the Post-Modern tradition. We see also the hallmarks of the Post-Modern project: being good without being utopian, accepting that there are no do-overs and learning from the environments that surround us.

The central section looks at the tactics, strategies and tropes of Radical Post-Modernism. Charles Jencks' essay 'Contextual Counterpoint' (pp 62–67) outlines a radical version of contextualism that expresses difference as well as continuity. Sean Griffiths writes about the figural section (pp 68–77), examining the various manifestations of the billboard and the mediated image within FAT's work. And Charles Holland looks at taste as a critical category, specifically in relation to class and how socioeconomic distinctions affect architectural meaning (pp 90–7).

The final section of the book deals with the historical legacy of Post-Modernism. Léa-Catherine Szacka's examination of the infamous 1980 Venice Biennale charts the battle between Post-Modernism's pluralist and historicist wings (pp 98–105). Kester Rattenbury reviews the specifically British tradition of 'PoMo' and the ideological battles of the 1980s that culminated in Venturi and Scott Brown's National Gallery Sainsbury Wing (pp 106–13). Finally, Eva Branscome looks at relationships between official and unofficial forms of urban placemaking through the role of graffiti (pp 114–21). Δ

Notes
1. Venturi appeared on the cover of the American magazine *Architecture*, of May 2001, with the words underneath his portrait 'I am not now and never have been a postmodernist', an ironic paraphrase of the way some intellectuals in the 1950s denied under oath that they were communists. The accompanying article was called 'A bas Postmodernism, of course,' leading to my letter and riposte that, like Groucho Marx, he 'would never join a club that would have him'.
2. Charles Jencks, *The Language of Post-Modern Architecture*, Academy Editions (London), 1977. The 7th edition is entitled *The New Paradigm in Architecture*, published by Yale University Press (New Haven and London), 2002.
3. Anthony Blunt, 'Some Uses and Abuses of the Terms Baroque and Rococo in Architecture', Oxford, 1973.
4. John Summerson said this to me on more than one occasion, and ended his influential *The Classical Language of Architecture* with the idea; see the 1980 edition, Thames & Hudson (London), p 114.
5. Dan Graham, 'Art in Relation to Architecture/Architecture in Relation to Art', in *Rock My Religion: Writings and Projects, 1965–90*, MIT Press (Cambridge, MA), 1993, pp 239–40.
6. David Harvey, *The Condition of Post Modernity: An Enquiry into the Origins of Cultural Change*, Blackwell (Cambridge, MA), 1990.
7. Gabriel Josipovici, *Whatever Happened to Modernism?*, Yale University Press (New Haven and London), 2010, pp 29–38.
8. Reinhold Martin, *Utopia's Ghost: Architecture and Postmodernism, Again*, University of Minnesota Press (Minnesota, MN), 2010, p xi.

Sam Jacob

BEYOND THE FLATLINE

High Post-Modernism with its understanding of the significance of the image anticipated the flattening of culture, first in advertising and the printed media, and more recently online. **Sam Jacob of FAT** speculates on architecture's relationship with the Internet, 'a flatland of undifferentiated information', and how Radical Post-Modernism might be best placed to resist the ubiquity of global culture while reanimating the social and cultural agenda of Modernism and Post-Modernism.

Marx argued that history repeats, first as tragedy, then as farce. But Marx never had cable TV or he would have watched history repeating endlessly. In the age of digital information, events come around again and again, their mode and meaning shifting with each cycle. Tragedy becomes farce and then spins into a dizzying blur of genres: Rom-Com, Family Drama, Satire, Pornography and so on. So Marx was half right. History repeats first as tragedy, then as farce, and then as tragi-farce-romcom-porno or slasher-drama-chic-flick-docudrama.

The same cultural trajectory holds true in architecture. Modernism ran its course as tragedy (heroic failure) while Post-Modernism acted out farce (ironic failure). After this, it – where 'it' means the historical trajectory of architectural culture – splinters into kaleidoscopic genre-Moderns: Neo-, Retro-, Alter-, Super-, Para- and Extra-Moderns. Porno-Modern, Slasher-Modern, Feelgood-Modern. Everything is flattened into an infinitely wide and depthless pool where image, text and history are dissolved by the solvents of media and communication. Not the end of history, but an intensifying and multiplying of histories into the present where we can be pre and post, neo and authentic simultaneously.

This cyclic turn is already inscribed in (early) Post-Modernism's attempts to reconnect architecture to the socially, politically and economically engaged ambitions of (early) Modernism – think, for example, of Denise Scott Brown's interest in what she describes as 'active socioplastics'. As Modernism recognised its early 20th-century industrial context, Post-Modernism resited late 20th-century architecture within the increasingly powerful context of globalisation, the growing ubiquity of media, liberalised markets and the free flow of capital, the pervasiveness of communication technology, the fragmentation of ideology, and so on.

While on one hand it attempted to reinvigorate Modernism's social programme, Post-Modernism simultaneously recognised the impossibility of constructing a utopian architectural programme. Indeed, it was often concerned with representing the impossibility of Utopia – or at least the contrast between the idealised and the everyday. Charles Moore's Piazza d'Italia in New Orleans, for example, invokes the Italian Renaissance in order to reveal contemporary culture's alienation from the values we associate with such ideals. Through what we might regard as this kind of intentionally farcical historicism, Post-Modernism signalled and signposted the reasons why the authentic Modernist project was doomed to tragic failure, and why its success could only ever exist as a zombified aesthetic.

High Post-Modernism's understanding of late 20th-century conditions anticipated the flattening of culture's structures. It not only told us this would happen (why else would it have been so invested in flatness of two dimensions?), how it would happen (media, advertising, cars and other consumerisms) and why it would happen (the ideology of late capitalism). It also knew that the mechanisms of culture would transform so radically that its own foundation would collapse, that its own critical position would too be flattened. Its ostentatious physical gestures were not waving but signalling a desperate truth at the moment before invisible torrents of neo-liberal, free market capitalism washed over everything. Post-Modernism's pluralism – once radical – has been co-opted as free market choice. The effects of fully fledged neo-liberal capitalism on our physical, social and economic landscapes is profound and disorientating. In the wake of such pretzel logics as credit default swaps – the standard-bearing instrument of deregulated, dematerialised financial product – we might add confusion to Post-Modernism's complexity and contradiction.

Now, when everything is one click away from everything else, high Post-Modernism's critical dialectic – the rhetoric of 'double coding' that allowed Post-Modernism to articulate its yes/no position – has exploded into multiple and provisional relationships. In our era of networked information, juxtapositions of high culture with popular, the historical with the contemporary or the academy with the everyday can no longer operate. Nodal points – Rome and Las Vegas, the temple and the shed, the pediment and the billboard – now bob in the flat pool of culture. Despite its interest in the everyday, the commercial and the ordinary, Post-Modern architecture's field of operation was within the academy, which like every other armature of culture has been flattened by neo-liberal ideology.

When Richard Hamilton's scissors chopped out an image of a lollipop with the word 'Pop' emblazoned on its wrapper from a magazine while composing *Just what is it that makes today's homes so different, so appealing?* (1956) as part of the 'This is Tomorrow' art/architecture exhibition, a trajectory was set that found architectural purchase in Post-Modernism a decade later. You can feel its tremors in Archigram, Ant Farm, Archizoom and certainly through Robert Venturi and Denise Scott Brown. 'Americans feel uncomfortable sitting in a square; they should be at home looking at television,' Venturi wrote (and then placed a golden TV aerial on top of his Guild House in Philadelphia (1961) as a monument to communication to make sure you knew how serious he was.[1] The radical gesture here was to cite the relationship between architecture, space and media – to speculate on what might happen iconographically or spatially if these two distinct worlds were to collide.

The 'tomorrow' that the Independent Group[2] speculated upon only partially materialised. Not the technological robot-assisted sci-fi, but the image-world of media that exploded with exceptional force and speed. Media, in our 'tomorrow', means networks of instantaneous communication create what we might call a collapsing of culture, meaning, geography and history – reconfiguring spatial relationships on the fly. The non-dimensional structure of the Internet alters our relationship to information. It lays out the entire repository of culture like a giant puddle, infinitely wide and without depth – a flatland of undifferentiated information. 'This' versus 'that' no longer exists. Instead 'this', 'that', 'them', 'those' and 'these' all happen simultaneously in a great horizontal flux.

From the Guggenheim Bilbao (1997) onwards, recent mainstream architectural avant-garde projects have used distorted (and depoliticised) abstractions of Modernist and Constructivist languages in ways that have suggested the clearest illustrations of the sensations of late capitalism: fluid form at audacious scale, the swoosh of volumes, the lightheadedness of reflection and translucencies, curves of overblown sensuality. This litany of effects formalises the heady liquid state of mind of millennial abstract-boom economics into physical and spatial form – literally sensational. While they accentuate Post-Modernism's sometime tendencies towards academic autonomy – the formal game – they have also removed its explicit critical and communicational position. That is to say, Post-Modernism has been, in some form, alive and well despite its apparent disappearance in a form we might name 'Complicit Post-Modernism'.

Radical Post-Modernism (RPM), however, is an alternative architectural approach that explicitly recognises the system within which architecture operates. Positioning itself between the mechanisms of globalisation and its effects on particular situations, it articulates a broader and nuanced understanding of architectural context. This can be seen in the charts and diagrams of networks that characterise its projects. Mappings of influences, agencies and the specifics of territories are not just research but become design tools. This concern for the intersection between networks and place, the overlapping of economic, legal, political and social realms with the physical environment is a way of defining an expanded idea of site and context within which architecture can operate.

RPM's contextual concern is also revealed in its propensity for detailed fieldwork and close reading of place rather than generalistion. Tracing the specifics of history, narratives of place, the particularities of occupation and the specifics of local activity and culture is a way of cataloguing moments of difference. These concerns act as a form of resistance to the ubiquity of global culture. They offer a means of inscribing particular narratives into the flatness and abstraction of generic urban planning.

RPM often reports from the places where the effects of contemporary culture are felt most: from border conditions, favelas, post-industrial regeneration, post-utopian new towns and rapidly expanding cities of emerging economies. These are places where the networks of economics, community, identity, history, power and politics have an exaggerated effect on the city.

This is a form of resistance, or perhaps more specifically a reintroduction of roughness, of non-slip texturing. Where neo-liberalism brings abstraction, this approach creates meaning. Where it atomises interests, this coalesces. It does this through

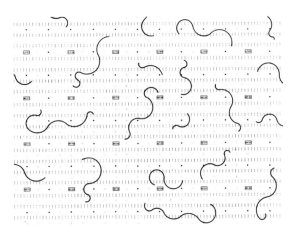

Radical Post-Modernism is in part radical because it addresses the scenarios of the 'real' directly. It is not *about* these conditions, but locates its practice *among* them.

uncovering, through speculating and creating fictions of significance, through inventing and inserting local loops into the wider network. While this argues for a conceptual position, it might also be seen in material and textural architectural formations. RPM's affinity with the ruin and the lumberyard talk of the realities of construction and attrition (of labour and time) rather than of the seamless formalism of digitally derived architectural formalism.

Radical Post-Modernism is in part radical because it addresses the scenarios of the 'real' directly. It is not *about* these conditions, but locates its practice *among* them. It does not extract the knowledge it 'learns from' to the cloisters of academia, but applies its learning within its own theatre of operation. Its politics and polemics are, therefore, more than rhetorical. Its radicalism, we could argue, originates from its practicality. Like singing into a vocoder, RPM's voice is polyphonic. Its discourse operates simultaneously across political, polemical and practical octaves.

The vernacular expression of flatlined culture is the mash-up. Here, cultural fragments crash into one another creating fleeting associations. We see YouTube videos that cut together videos of piano-playing cats to form the entirety of Arnold Schoenberg's *Drei Klavierstücke*. We see films redubbed, images cut together in amateurish Photoshop, songs of different genres spliced. In each case, things which apparently had different meanings – things that made them distinct – suddenly become synchronised. The tactics of avant-garde art practice – collage, juxtaposition and appropriation – have become the foundation of cultural practice in the age of the Internet. The lolcat is the inheritor of a cultural heritage that stretches back to the Cabaret Voltaire. Marx's historical repetitions flicker like a zoetrope, their multiple images blurred into singular visual persistence.

Radical Post-Modernism's context is a function of these phenomena, where images, references, history and values click, click, click into multiple arrangements. The flatness of the network opens up cultural production as a practice of reorganising existing information into provisional constellations. It reworks found models, remaking and remodelling imagery in ways that create new meanings. If RPM sites itself within this landscape, it also appropriates the phenomena, the tools and the tactics of the flatland as its methods of its operation. Flatlands tactics are re-employed as a means of critique.

For example, we might consider the returning significance of the communicative surface in architecture.

The dominant mode of an information glutted, mediated culture is the image. Image, information and communication are everyday, immersive experiences that work us over completely without respite. Architecture too plays its part in this image culture, but often implicitly. Its various modes of operation – functional, sculptural, ecological and so on – produce image as by-product.

But following the pretzel logic of late capitalism, if architecture-as-image is the condition demanded by late-capitalist culture then resistance might be contained by explicitly constructing architectural imagery. Architecture's surface here is not something that acts as a camouflage behind which self-interest flows in secret, but rather a surface as the site where ideologies are acted out in plain view. By re-engaging with explicit communication, architecture can develop its imaging quality as a tool to engage with the cultures within which it finds itself rather than simply in the service of culture.

What is at stake here is the value of meaning, which in itself is a radical position in relationship to the endlessly abstract machinations of mainstream architecture. Abstraction, we might argue, operates as a function of neo-liberalist desire to reduce everything to market terms by removing signifying qualities that locate work in any specific context. Radical Post-Modernism's desire to manufacture meaning addressing identity, class, taste and so on asserts other cultural and political values. The construction of meaning becomes an act of resistance, its methods of constructing particular versions of publicness.

At its most potent, the narrative content of RPM is derived from its close reading of its theatre of operation and its attunement to the intersections of interests that occur in any given site. Architecture becomes a surface through which these narratives can be publicly understood and articulated. Its ability to manufacture speculative narratives becomes a way of creating new forms of publicness and new associations of community.

In the flatlands of networked culture there is a perverse Pop-will-eat-itself aspect to Post-Modernism's reappearance.

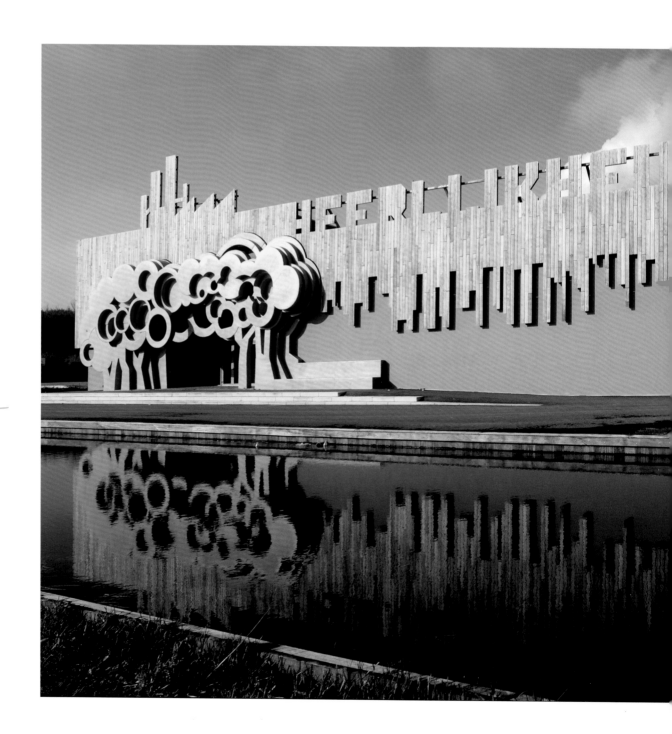

In effect, image performs architecturally. Cut loose by the associative and provisional nature of images in a networked world, architecture unleashes its kaleidoscopic Moderns: Black Villa Savoyes, ruins as ironic celebrations of regeneration, generic industrial structures retooled to tell stories specific to a particular community.

In the flatlands of networked culture there is a perverse Pop-will-eat-itself aspect to Post-Modernism's reappearance. But more significantly, its return, outside of its historical moment, potentially allows its programme to be manifest. It can be released from the parochial arguments of grey and white, high and low, tradition and modernity that swirled around it and eventually drove it into the sand. If we are not at the end of history and we are outside the vectors of progressive Marxian historical materialism then here, beyond the flatline, we might escape both farce and tragedy. Through embracing the multiplicity of genres and the collapse of traditional ordering of time that characterises the flatland, perhaps RPM can operate not as a doomed opposition to the failure of Modernism, but as a way of reanimating Modern and Post-Modern concerns simultaneously.

Ironically, the reinterrogation of a mode of practice characterised by the inauthentic is surprising. This simulation of simulation that should result in an overload of irony seems to create instead a deep sincerity. It might help us to conceive of the discipline of architecture as an active social and cultural practice that is located within particular contexts and constraints while critically engaged with the flatlined nature of contemporary culture as the site of its operation. ∆

Notes

1. Robert Venturi, *Complexity and Contradictions in Architecture*, Museum of Modern Art (New York), 1966, p 131.
2. The Independent Group consisted of painters, sculptors, architects, writers and critics active in London from 1952 to 1956. Their interests in the aesthetics of mass culture and a 'found object' aesthetic challenged prevailing Modernist approaches to culture. Members included Alison and Peter Smithson, Reyner Banham, Eduardo Paolozzi and Richard Hamilton.

RADICAL POST-MODERNISM AND CONTENT

CHARLES
JENCKS

AND

REM
KOOLHAAS

DEBATE THE ISSUE

The following debate took place on 28 December 2009 between **Charles Jencks** and **Rem Koolhaas,** and was transcribed and edited by Eva Branscome. Jencks and Koolhaas have exchanged ideas since the late 1960s. Jencks was the one to insist that Koolhaas come to the 1980 Venice Biennale, originally entitled 'Post-Modernism'. (Paolo Portoghesi invited Jencks to collaborate with him on this first Biennale before it expanded into historicism.) In January 2002, Jencks was also a judge of the competition for the CCTV Building, the headquarters for China Central Television in Beijing, discussed below. Jencks and Koolhaas continue to thrive on their discussions and disagreements. Although they have very different commitments to the issue of 'content', their varying positions help to clarify what is meant here by 'radical'.

THE 1980 VENICE BIENNALE: REVIVING SURREALISM

Charles Jencks: With the recent move back to Post-Modernism, that is, back to the future of the past, I want to focus on the radical part of the equation: on content, narrative and communication. This was the kind of Post-Modernism that you and I were interested in. When you came to the Venice Biennale in 1980, you produced a facade that was slightly a Modernist revival, but how would you position it?

Rem Koolhaas: I was uncomfortable with the notion of this street, 'Strada Novissima' and the title 'The Presence of the Past', and I was working with Stefano de Martino on that. Even the obligation to design a facade was difficult – but you were the one that always told me that I could do facades, so …

CJ: And you believed that?

RK: Yeah, I believed that – it's an impossibility around which I had to construct my whole career. Nevertheless, the interior of our space showed a very serious effort to deal with 'the presence of the past' because it featured the Hague Parliament, and that scheme was about opening up a medieval fortress to a democratic process and doing it in a very demonstrative and aesthetic way. There was a breach in the walls of the fortress and in that breach stepped several architectural elements and courtyards. It was the first time that we were actually involved in preservation, which has now become one of our dominant themes. So it may be one of those cases where I thought I didn't belong, but in the end belonged much more than I thought.

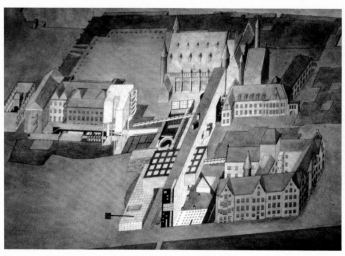

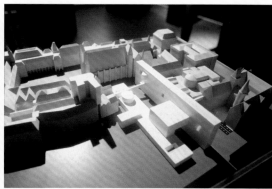

CJ: Your project was a kind of 'subversion from within', one of the general 1970s definitions of Post-Modernism, that is, reusing the system in a way that isn't its usual purpose. In that sense you're breaching the walls, you're using preservation to send a different message from Prince Charles, are you?

RK: It was a kind of serious preoccupation with the past in any case. The message could have been about opening up and perforating the wall, probably very naïve, but we called it our 'new sobriety'.

CJ: 'New Sobriety', because you were going against the other Post-Modernists in the Biennale?

RK: Yes, but in retrospect I think that I did not go against anything. And so in retrospect I have a much more modest …

CJ: You're retrospectively being modest?

RK: No, I'm being more inclusive, or being more sceptical of being independent of other things that were obviously going on. And also in retrospect I've benefited enormously from all the things I was supposedly against.

CJ [laughs]: You're in your Late-Mellow Period, but your new sobriety was a kind of Neo-Miesian and Ungers' Minimalism.

RK: I was definitely seduced by their kind of virtuosity. Maybe you could construct an argument that our whole work is a kind of desperate standoff between the generic and virtuosity. Virtuosity that has no place inside the generic and that has to find a place.

CJ: Your facades are a cross between boxes and icons.

RK: Yeah they hide virtuosity sometimes, or sometimes they're not boxes at all. There's one more thing about the Biennale facade. There was a neon sign that emerged at right angles to the facade and of course in one direction it said OMA, but in the other direction it said AMO – so there was already a kind of awareness.

CJ: You hadn't foreseen inventing the 1998 AMO, the interest in content?

RK: No, but I was aware that it meant 'I love' in Italian or in Latin.

CJ: '*Amo, amas, amat*', the first words one learns in Latin 101.

RK: Yeah. So that was at least a game.

CJ: The neon sign, the whiteness, the sail, the cantilever and the pin – all of those tropes were within the International Style crossed with Surrealism, and the 1950s biomorphic.

RK: Exactly.

CJ: So you were reviving the recent past, the presence of the past for you was Surrealism.

RK: Yeah, and Wallace Harrison the kind of corporate decadence that also was very close to Surrealism – his UN building, it's full of surreal moments.

CJ: Very hard-headed Surrealism.

OMA, Casa da Musica, Porto, 2002–5
Views, plans and analyses of some metaphors found by critics and
the public. Drawings by Madelon Vriesendorp.

RK: And also very strange effects.

CJ: Open for you as a European to see; but for Americans, like me, impossible, because we see the corporate grin of idiocy.

RK: Yet Harrison was completely obsessed by Europe – he worked with Le Corbusier and Léger. I organised a show at the Institute (IAUS, New York) on Harrison in 1979, a year before the Venice Biennale.

CJ: And you wrote *Delirious New York* in 1978, which you can read as a kind of Post-Modern psychoanalysis of New York.

RK: Completely. Anyway, *Delirious New York* is definitely not an argument for Modernity.

THE ICONIC BUILDING AND RADICAL POST-MODERNISM

CJ: It is an argument for scriptwriting, and for your finding a secret narrative behind New York. Yet, given your Miesian love of the box and the newly sober, you have approached the genre of the iconic building through the back door. The Casa da Musica in Porto is definitely an icon for the city and won the competition because it was seen in metaphorical terms as 'a diamond that fell from the sky'. At least that's how the press saw it, as a kind of geological mineral. My argument in *The Iconic Building: The Power of Enigma*, is that such natural and cosmic content is the sometimes hidden code for the recent tradition going back to Ronchamp.

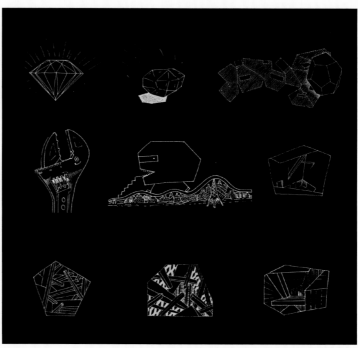

RK: That brings up an interesting historical point. It's a serious mistake to look at just the last 15 years as the emergence of the iconic. You have to look at the whole postwar period, Saarinen's TWA Terminal and Ronchamp, or any amount of other such buildings. You could even instance Mies' National Gallery in Berlin, really much more indebted to that tradition than Minimalism. I am really horrified how 'iconic' has now become an entirely negative tag.

CJ: But only within the architectural profession, of puritans and Minimalists. Among the public, when it's done well, it's still extremely popular and that is why communication is so important to this issue on *Radical Post-Modernism*. A building has to be content-driven to be radical today, and that content must be public and significant.

RK: In communication the iconic image is unbelievably important. Now we have a curious moment where we're working on a Hong Kong project with a very large team of several cultural personalities. One of them, Hans Ulrich Obrist, is a curator of the Serpentine Gallery. Even they know our project has to be iconic – it's like a nightmare.

CJ: You're damned if you do, and you're damned if you don't.

RK: We all know the evil aura of the word. I prefer to read 'iconic' simply as 'opposed to Second World War architecture'.

CJ: Again – the presence of the recent past.

RK: Yes, and outside the West – for instance, if you look at Russian architecture of the 1970s and 80s – in Tashkent. It was in the same kind of tradition as the Germans and Americans at the time.

CJ: The same bloodline. Porto, I've analysed, with Madelon's drawings, as the interaction of multiple metaphors. Not only 'the diamond that fell from the sky', the 'wrench' and 'pacman', but as 'the route building with Piranesian space'. These mixed metaphors heighten perception as one winds up the spatial route to the top, the culmination – the 'dangerous optical illusion', the Bridget Riley connecting us to the overall view of the city. One of its wonderful merits is the dramatic contrast of the route, a series of dark forbidding spaces followed by cuts of brilliant light that reveal a glimpse of Porto. Then, at the top, is this suicidal roof deck with its diagonal grid that appears to leap over the wall (the glass fence is invisible). The paranoia of such optical tricks combines with the slightly sinister overtones of the pacman (the kind of instrument that would eat up the city). Like some of Norman Foster's more bizarre mechanistic icons, the overall image of the building is like a piece of white engineering, a blown-up hairdryer, or a computer accessory. It's sinister in some respects, stern and forbidding in a way that Portuguese cathedrals are cold on the outside and hot on the inside.

RK: Can I add a few adjectives? In my view of an iconic reading, it is both strong and weak, and in that sense it has a lot in common with our CCTV building. This is also, from certain angles, really impressive, and from other angles completely and deliberately unimpressive. That explains their oscillating relationship with the context, which it sometimes consumes and to which it sometimes gives. So I would not emphasise only the coldness or the hardness.

CJ: But would you agree that it is cold, tough, urban, severe, Calvinist?

RK: No.

CJ: OK, I'm wrong, but I love it partly because it has this Portuguese severity. The Portuguese can be very tough, black and white. After all, it's the land of Álvaro Siza and Paula Rego.

> **RK:** Of course it was really interesting to assume a Portuguese identity. But I would not call it a Protestant – if anything, it is more a Catholic building.

CJ: And also Catholic, or multiple-coded on the inside, with three different kinds of Portuguese tiles. So, it's a Radical Post-Modern building in the sense that it communicates on many levels, and to many different kinds of people. Its interior theatres, while severely geometric, are also sensuously decorative and with funny touches and details. As an iconic, mixed metaphor it is like the CCTV building which used Chinese icons in an enigmatic way; it relates to Chinese puzzles, the Chinese moon gate, the Chinese emphasis on bracket construction, the spider's web of structure The government client wanted an icon, and they explicitly asked for one. The other 11 competitors, however, gave us just one more skyscraper in an area that will have 300 and, the jury that I was on, took your point that the 301st skyscraper would not be an icon. So you understood perfectly what they needed, a kind of 'anti-skyscraper'. But this brings up the question: who is the audience for which it is iconic – with whom do you want to communicate?

> **RK:** Definitely not architects, but to some extent the clients, and of course more than anything the public at large.

CJ: Who would that be?

> **RK:** In Porto both the users and the people who are outside the building. One of the virtues in Porto is that you can be a participant without even being inside.

CJ: Certainly, as I found, taxi drivers in both Porto and in Beijing love your buildings and have it on their mobile phones. They could take you to them quickly and give you the usual gossip about them. I heard about the campaign against you in China, partly driven by jealous architects and others, who have wilfully interpreted your building as pornographic, as a 'pants building'. That is a mad, paranoiac metaphor really, because try as most Westerners do they cannot decode the pants.

> **RK:** It is mad.

CJ: It is crazy, but a truth of all icons is that they have to be attacked by iconoclasts. Do you want to speak to that critique?

> **RK:** It was unfortunate that we contributed to it by publishing the rejected covers of our AMO magazine in *Content* itself. *Content* was a 'bookazine' in which we tried to talk about architecture as if it were a light-hearted subject. So we did these suggestive cartoons and did a lot to eliminate the heavy seriousness of usual architecture. But I've been able to rectify the misunderstanding in China.

CJ: Well, an icon will be a lightning rod for people who don't agree with you. How could it be otherwise? Yet, like Le Corbusier, you sometimes publish negative reviews of your own work along with the presentation, a virtually unique practice for the iconic architect. This is to admit the very deep truth that, if you do like something, you also reserve the right for other people to hate it, the truth of taste and emotion as being essential freedoms and essential preconditions for architectural meaning.

RK: I had to go on TV in China about this porno issue, and one of our strongest counterarguments was the discovery of an anonymous poem. It was written by a steel worker, on one of the beams – an incredibly moving poem about his pride in building. It answered the pants metaphor quite effectively.

CJ: When I climbed out on the top of CCTV, I was so moved by it as a piece of steel construction. The architecture is built all the way through, whereas in America probably they would have cheated on the top, not have put in real steel. This obsession illustrates your AA Thesis, 'Voluntary Prisoners of Architecture', the excessive dedication to the craft, the Miesian love of the I-beam and dark Miesian skin. Yet you also play the structural truth game with PM irony. For instance, where you don't need the beams coming down the skin near the ground, you just subtract them, you dissolve the diagrid, – beautiful!

RK: I'm very proud of that.

CJ: And credit for that goes to your engineer?

RK: Credit for that goes to the collaboration between Cecil Balmond and me.

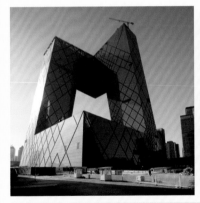

THE GENERATIVE SECTION AND THE ROUTE BUILDING

CJ: The organisational diagram and the routes through a building are two motives you share with Le Corbusier (*le promenade architectural*). Your Seattle Library, the Dutch Embassy in Berlin, Porto and CCTV are all route buildings – what about these motives?

> **RK:** I'm a little embarrassed because it seems kind of a default to have to give these justifications. But, in certain cases such as the Dutch Embassy, there were strong arguments that a route needed to be the driving force. The diplomats needed an accessible conversation piece for visitors, and that is how it works to perfection; they are convinced the route makes their work easier.

CJ: As they saunter up and take people through, they converse easily about the changing scenes?

> **RK:** They converse about the sheer difference of encounters with recent history, displayed on the walls. For instance, the convenient 12-minute inspections of communism, of capitalism and Catholicism, and of Nazism. The whole pictorial panorama is unfolded on the route. It's partly a coincidence that these are four route buildings, but that has everything to do with their public nature. One of the great ironies of my building versus my writing is that I've theorised all about a kind of architecture that I've rarely done myself.

CJ: Eh?

> **RK:** Well, we have prepared for architecture in the age of modernisation, in the age of capitalism. But actually what we've done is traditional and classic public buildings. And so it's opened up a huge gap. Ironically part of my reputation as a cynic is based on the more theoretical side, but if you look at the built work it's so earnest it makes you cry how (un)cynical it is.

CJ: Exactly, but also the Seattle building is actually an icon and another mixed metaphor of the earth, of the mineral, of 'congested culture', of superposition. And its organisation is really radical, the generative section, and comes from a famous diagram: the Big Mac sandwich diagram.

> **RK:** The cleverness is that it started with an analysis of those parts of the building that were going to be unstable programmatically and those parts that could be assumed to be relatively fixed all the time. That opposition developed two totally different architectures for the model. One is highly organised, and the other loose and casual. So between the slices of the sandwich is room to evolve and find alternate layers.

CJ: Rather Metabolist.

> **RK:** Yes, of course I was stunned by how close some of the things were with the Japanese movement.

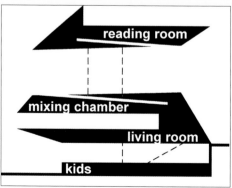

Rem Koolhaas with AMO, Eneropa Project, April 2010
The images show energy interdependency between regions optimising their
specific ecological advantages. Note the new regional names and alliances,
nations redivided up along lines suitable to each energy condition (Tidal
States and Isles of Wind, Solaria for Spain/Italy, Geothermalia, Biomassburg).

CONTENT: REBRANDING THE EU AND THE AMBIGUITY OF POWER

CJ: Returning to content, our interests have come together over things like Robert Venturi, and branding, especially your work on the E-Conology for the EU. When did you start the EU project?

RK: I remember because we presented the report on 12 September 2001.

CJ [laughs]: It must have disappeared.

RK: Yeah, and it was more interesting because some EU leaders were convinced that the Americans had created 9/11.

CJ: They had a conspiracy theory?

RK: Almost without exception, and we were all really taken aback. In any case, our EU thinking has gone through three phases. One was a deliberate investigation of the iconographic deficit, an attempt to try to find a language to explain it, to make the EU project more attractive. The second one was an exhibition on Europe that we did in 2004 or 2005 in Brussels, on the history of Europe, and the third one, which I'm doing now, as part of a group of 10 thinkers, tries to define the European Union in 2030. So I went from working on icons to working on shaping. The group includes Lech Walesa, and the former prime minister of Spain who led Spain from fascism into democracy. So it's a really interesting group leading to a Euro project we're making public in May.

What I'm focused on is their need to see the EU from outside Europe because it has been desperately introverted, over the past 10 years, and been oblivious of how it comes across and how it expects its exceptional complexities to be accommodated by the rest of the world. So I've collected a lot of evidence from outside Europe to introduce it here. For instance Kishore Mahbubani, the Singapore diplomat, who is an incredible critic of Europe. So I'm basically working with Europe's critics to try to filter some of their observations into the process. That is because I have a vast international experience which is kind of interesting.

Rem Koolhaas/AMO, European Bar Code for the EU, 2002 and
Charles Jencks, New EU Flag Design, 2007
Jencks' flag design is based on the original 12 stars and the
Koolhaas bar code.

CJ: The critical as part of the radical: you've begun to get a double view of the EU.

RK: Yeah. Really.

CJ: When you presented it in 2005 at the panoramic exhibition, was it a kind of double coding of tastes, one of the ideas and tactics of Post-Modernism?

RK: Yes, the exhibition showed a history of Europe in two ways. The outer ring of the panorama depicted the actual history of Europe, starting with the Romans, but it also included fascism, Bolshevism etc. And then the inner ring showed the history of the EU, so you always could see them both together, since the inner panorama was lower in height than the outer. The present project, with the group of 10 thinkers, samples a number of criticisms of how Europe behaves, from places like Dubai, Abu Dhabi, Singapore and China.

CJ: You're bringing an international point of view to what is a new kind of empire. Robert Cooper in his book *Breaking of Nations* calls the EU 'a voluntary empire'. He divides political formations into pre-modern states, or the failed states; then the modern states, like Iraq, and then the very very modern evolving states such as America; and finally the Post-Modern formations like the EU. A modern state is based on hard power, centralised production, and the biggest standing armies and defence systems. In Post-Modern, soft-power states, Cooper puts the regional groupings, such as ASEAN but particularly the EU. He talks about Europe as 'a cooperative empire' of 27 nations that join voluntarily, and he uses Mark Leonard's metaphor of it being like a Visa card. As an empire it's a very small head on an extra large torso, but it's an enabling body for the 27 nations. They create unity by having 80,000 rules! So Mark Leonard, your friend and one adviser, calls it *the* system for the 21st century. To most of the world this body looks invisible, so your role has been to try to give it presence and an e-conology: in effect, to brand it. Your branding with the bar code, for instance – how did you come to the bar code?

RK: Basically the fear of Europe partly results from the fact that none of the leaders has actually explained the reason for the conception of Europe to the population. That creates a fear of losing national identity, so we tried to find a way of articulating the larger whole without abandoning the identity of the individual partners. The bar code seemed the most efficient way of doing that, and ironically it's something that everyone understands immediately.

CJ: Many people, including me, say that the bar code doesn't give much individuality. It may give the minimal, linear colours of a flag, but it actually subverts national identity behind the commercial metaphor, the triumph of the economy over nationhood. So, although there is plurality in the great number of colours, the check-out code is a bit nasty as a total metaphor. Have other people reacted this way?

RK: No, I think it's a fair comment. But, on the other hand it's a little bit far-fetched and I think that it's so cheerful.

CJ: Like the cheerfulness of your Edwardian tent for the EU exhibit, with its multiple colours, the feeling of going out to see a rowing event. The cheerfulness overcomes the commercial?

RK: Attempts to transcend the commercial …

CJ: As you know, I stole your design and made a new, improved version of the EU flag, which has yet to be accepted. It shows a rising, blue sun, exploding over the world, and yet it keeps the original 12 stars, the unity of where it came from, rather like the American flag with its original 13 stars; and of course it was partly derived from your bar code.

RK: Can I steal it back?

CJ: Yeah, please. My version is somehow less commercial and still pluralist.

RK: And a little bit more Japanese.

CJ: The stars are rising, so the past and the various colours are both embedded in it.

RK: Actually our bar code has been used intermittently, once by the kind of Austrian presidency, and now I guess we are facing a moment of truth where we could see whether we should make an all-out push to have it part of the real currency or not.

CJ: For conservative reasons EU leaders are regressing to the 12 stars. They don't want to give it up for fear of finding something worse. Typically today the EU has this unnameable head who no one can remember.

RK: Rompuy.

CJ: Except you.

RK: That's all part and parcel of the invisibility agenda, the stealth situation, and the interpretation of it as a kind of Post-Modern empire actually makes sense. The problem is that this mission has been so sloppily managed, but if you use stealth as a kind of metaphor then 'penetration' is obviously crucial, and I think that the last decade of total preoccupation with procedures has kind of interrupted the process of exchange and penetration.

CJ: Are you saying the cult of personality has destroyed a lot of national politics and this is a positive cult of impersonality?

RK: Partly. The concept of syndicated legislation could still work, provided it were efficient and they were smart enough to negotiate cleverly. It's true if you track the number of rules that are adopted even by people who don't want to be part of the EU. It's amazing that, for instance, in order to trade, South America is adopting European rules; and in order to trade, Africa is adopting European rules. So, more and more we are providing the laws that organise all the interactions. And so if we really focused on that, it could be an incredibly productive thing. Or the blueprints for Copenhagen, crafting the international framework without necessarily pushing it.

CJ: Stealth, rules of the road, bureaucratic rules, trading rules, rules of a club, the Club of Europe …

RK: The interesting thing is that they are no longer just the rules of the club, but simply the rules of any transaction between partners that have nothing to do with Europe.

CJ: Like Visa card. You're putting it forward as a kind of universal earth rule.

RK: Not rule …

CJ: But they *are* rules that you have to follow, or at least pretend that you are following, like Romania. But, one of the reasons that some people of Britain are so critical and sceptical is that other nations don't obey the rules. We know they cheat …

RK: I think there is always a political override. Basically Romania had to be made a member for political reasons, and I still think that it's working out – slowly but surely.

CJ: I'm pro-European but critical. Architecturally speaking the EU's bureaucratic production is really second-rate, PoMo not Radical Post-Modern.

RK: Really embarrassing.

CJ: It's handed out as pork-barrel, as 'jobs for the boys'. As e-conology the main sculpture by the front door is excruciating, a young Western woman trampling on an Eastern slave, as she holds the sign of the currency triumphantly in salute – 'Euro über alles'. It makes one cringe for the idea of Europe. The Court of Human Rights by Richard Rogers, or the new parliament building suffer from bureaucratic elephantiasis. The Euro-fudge of most symbolism is appalling. Take the money, the 5-euro note, which castrates its model, the real Pont du Gard, or the 10-euro note that emasculates an existing French bridge – everything is watered down.

RK: Everything is more generic.

CJ: You say generic, I say 'mid-cult' or 'glob-cult'. When I criticised the EU architecture to Mark Leonard at his public lecture he responded that the 40 buildings they inhabit are rented! This is the typical quisling riposte that, if they don't own them, they're not responsible. So they turn the centre of Brussels into a 'nowheresville' of *rentier* space, and argue it's the landlords what done it.

RK: That is complete nonsense. They didn't make a contribution either positive or negative to the centre of Brussels. The centre of Brussels was basically a developers' area.

CJ: Surely they have a responsibility for the EU area, and around their non-centre they have allowed, right next to them, these historic places to crumble. It is a cynical piece of architectural misdirection.

RK: What do you mean?

CJ: I've walked the major buildings, probably as you have, and seen their countenance. As Ruskin would say, if you judge a culture by its architecture, then the face of the EU is at a stage of premature decadence.

RK: It's true and obvious, we identified that as a major issue. Although the EU may be the most important subject we have dealt with, as you say, our work here is very modest. That's how I would rather formulate it.

CJ: In your book on *Content* you have a section, 'Go East', and go with Europe as opposed to America. But can we talk about *Content* per se, that is more the work of AMO than it is of OMA, right?

RK: It's mixed.

CJ: Anyway, and funnily enough, you mentioned at the same time as Norman Foster that architects have little power. But I know that, from time to time, you get exercised by the fact that pop stars and iconic artists command much more money than architects. So, in this context of money and power, I would comment on the odd coincidence that both you and Norman are now working in the Middle East, doing these new ecological cities that look rather similar. And you simultaneously come up with the fact that you architects are virtually powerless.

RK: No. I always said that there's a mixture of omnipotence and impotence, a poisonous oscillation between the two.

CJ: Because you're omnipotent when you're getting the job and then impotent when it starts?

RK: No. It's not a linear, sequential thing, and sometimes at the end, or in the middle, power comes back.

CJ: In what way are you impotent?

RK: Well, it's more about not being able to define your own content. It's very obvious that anyone who waits and essentially spends his life waiting has a kind of curious relationship with the passive. Let me put it that way.

CJ: So unlike a painter and a sculptor who initiates …

RK: You cannot put your own agenda first …

CJ: Or a writer …

RK: You're kind of stuck.

CJ: So you always have to wait to be asked to dance.

RK: Yeah.

CJ: While you do propose a lot of programmatic content, you are saying you're impotent about really designing the iconography?

RK: Of course you have limited possibilities, but once you've been asked to dance you can achieve a lot in whatever direction you want to aim. It is basically the waiting game, and then the inability to control the process to the end, that hurts. Because you don't have money and executive power, you're dependent. At first you're dependent on the initiative of somebody else, then you're dependent on the economy, and then the politics and …

CJ: In the past the client knew what a building was about and would hire artists and other ancillary trades and practices to carry out a socially shared vision. Isn't that why collaboration with artists and other media is essential if you want a complete building? I don't think a building has this kind of autonomy that it can complete itself.

RK: Maybe you're right, but collaboration does not work with artists the way the system currently works. I, of course, have an incredible nostalgia for the condition of the *Gesamtkunstwerk*. It would require a lot of sharing and the current culture has an absolute phobia of sharing.

CJ: The present system may have this phobia, but your work seems to be crossing the boundaries, jumping the categories and in that sense it continues the radical agenda of Post-Modernism. Crossing the gap, jumping the fence was the PoMo phrase, 'operating in the gap between art and life', and that seems to me what you're doing.

RK: So we are trying to develop our own initiatives and to develop on a really modest scale our own powers. ∆

A FIELD GUIDE TO RADICAL POST-MODERNISM

Sean Griffiths, Charles Holland and Sam Jacob of FAT curate and classify the work of a diverse and international grouping of Radical Post-Modern architects. They range from the recently defunct Foreign Office Architects (FOA), known for their proclivity for pattern and ornament, to Tokyo-based Atelier Bow-Wow, who are rigorous in their pursuit of the ordinary. They run the gamut of the highly figurative, as exemplified by Melbourne-based practice ARM, to the expressive austerity of Swiss architect Valerio Olgiati.

The following pages showcase the work of 10 current practitioners whose work explores aspects of Radical Post-Modernism. They are both big and small, critical and commercial, consciously and unconsciously working within a Post-Modern tradition. Some – like CUP and Crimson – are not architects at all, but are critically involved in the creation of architecture and urbanism.

In the best Post-Modernism tradition we have corralled this diverse collection into a matrix (opposite), a taxonomy of RPM values, tactics and tropes. In some cases the work of the selected practitioners applies only to one or two of these values; in other cases many of them do. The point is that no one is wholly radically Post-Modern, and the matrix represents a shifting set of values rather than a straightforward manifesto. You can be in *and* out at the same time, an occasional binge drinker at the fountain of PoMo or a habitual but moderate imbiber and everything in between.

The matrix is, therefore, both expansive and reductive, absurd and acute. It is consciously limiting and elliptical, allowing shades of grey as well as emphatic answers. ***AD***

MATRIX OF RADICAL POST-MODERNISM

RADICAL POST-MODERNISM PRACTITIONERS

		RADICAL POST-MODERNISM VALUES											
		formal tropes				communication					social content		
		imitation	fragmentation	figural section	collage	counterpoint contextualism	iconography	ornamentation	double coding	ordinariness / the everyday	critique / polemic	pluralism	collaboration
ironic	ARM	●	·		●	○			·		·	●	
	Atelier Bow-Wow	·				●	○			●	·		○
	John Körmeling	●		·		●	·		○	○			·
activist	Crimson					○	·			●	●	●	●
	CUP									●	○	●	●
	muf	·	○		●	●	·	·	○	●	●	○	●
narrative	FAT	●		●	○	●					●	·	·
	Édouard François	●	·	○	●	●			·				
	Terunobu Fujimori	●					·			●			
	Hild und K	●	·	·		●	●	·	·				
un-ironic	Caruso St John	●		·	●	●	·		○		○	·	·
	FOA								●		●		
	Valerio Olgiati		·					·	●				

The questions such work raises centre around issues of authenticity, authorship and originality. These shibboleths of artistic production have long been questioned in fine art, but rarely in architecture. However, the borrowing, or reuse, of existing objects is a key tactic of Radical Post-Modernism. By using objects invented for another place and time, copying asserts an interest in the cultural meaning of architecture over technocratic or functionalist concerns. In fact, it subverts the myths of functionalism and technical efficiency as much as it does those of artistic originality and individual genius.

ARM's work, as evidenced in the practice's recent Royal Melbourne Institute of Technology (RMIT) building, also has a cartoonish quality, using figurative elements that challenge the tasteful restraint that characterises much architectural production. Authenticity, abstraction, authorship and taste: ARM's work attacks all these taboos with a brazen lack of restraint.

Melbourne-based ARM's work is provocatively unoriginal. Their projects employ sampling – the collaging of various existing examples of high architecture – in a way that is analogous to digitally produced dance music. The most audacious example of this is the presence of a slick, black copy after Le Corbusier's Villa Savoye within their National Museum of Australia (2001). The museum is, in fact, a series of copies, a whole album's worth of cover versions featuring, alongside Le Corbusier, Daniel Libeskind, Frank Gehry and Charles Moore. It is part barefaced cheek and part lopsided homage.

ARM, National Museum of Australia, Canberra, 2001
above: The unmistakable twisted geometry of Berlin's Jewish Museum is 'borrowed' from Daniel Libeskind and transported across the globe, coming to rest in the leafy peninsula of Canberra.

ARM, Australian Institute of Aboriginal and Torres Strait Islander Studies, Canberra, 2001
opposite top: The Villa Savoye in negative. A copy of Le Corbusier's most famous villa emerges from the facade of this building, its white render replaced by slick, black cladding panels.

ARM, Building 22, Royal Melbourne Institute of Technology (RMIT), Melbourne, 2010
opposite bottom: 'Greenwash' as designed by Walt Disney. Vivid, ultra-real bits of vegetation grow over the existing library building of the university to create a new rooftop space.

Valerio Olgiati

At first glance, Swiss architect Valerio Olgiati's work seems anything but Post-Modern. The majority of his buildings are austerely minimal, deliberately mute and enigmatic objects that sit aloof from context and apart from concerns with architectural style. His buildings, however, have always played games with their own austere imagery, hiding labyrinthine and perverse interiors within their cubic forms. Lately he has begun to use more ornamental and decorative forms too. His design for the Perm Museum in Russia (2008) is a series of stacked boxes cloaked by an ornamental screen made up of upside-down arches. The arches form an abstracted tracery, reminiscent of more ancient, pre-modern forms of architecture. The apartments of the Ardia Palace in Albania (2008) are draped in a similar concrete veil, like a petrified, lace tablecloth.

The use of decorative elements – albeit at a disembodied and highly ambiguous scale – links Olgiati's work to Post-Modernism's interest in ornament and pattern. The interiors of his buildings explore some of Post-Modernism's interest in fragmented and layered spaces too, often involving a deliberate disinterest in function. This ambiguous interest in typology and ahistorical forms links his work to the Swiss/Italian Tendenza school. Externally, his buildings are anti-contextual in a way that expresses a strange otherworldliness, appearing to be part of some forgotten or alien language of architecture.

Valerio Olgiati, Ardia Palace, Tirana, Albania, 2008
above: Swathes of concrete hang like a giant patterned tablecloth over an enigmatic block of apartments.

Valerio Olgiati, Perm Museum XXI, Perm, Russia, 2008
opposite top: A series of monumental stacked blocks are again cloaked in a draped concrete tracery that makes the building look at once familiar and alien.

Valerio Olgiati, Visitors Centre, Swiss National Park Centre, Zernez, Switzerland, 2008
opposite bottom: Interior view showing the bifurcated stairway. Pragmatic functionalism is challenged through the duplication of routes and a highly ambiguous hierarchy of spaces.

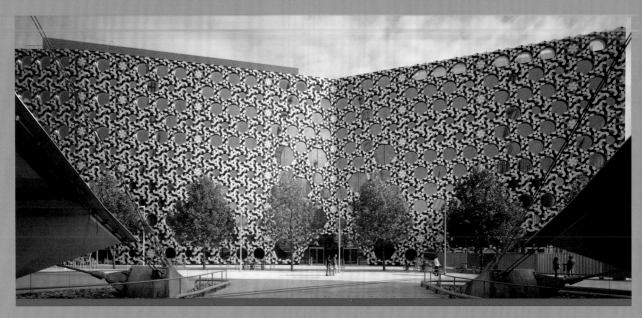

Somewhere beyond the diagram, the politics of the envelope, the function of ornament, FOA retasked its approach. Recalling Post-Modernism's 'pattern all over', the surfaces of FOA become inscribed with often eye-popping Op Art patterns. This reworking of the architects' origins as a post-OMA practice suggests a kind of epiphany that occurred at the limits of their commercial outreach – that the encounter with the realities of clients and publics led to a new understanding of the ways in which architecture performs. At the same time, their projects often use the idea of metaphor – the wave in the case of the Yokohama Ferry Terminal (2002), or muscle in the case of their early proposal for the London Olympics stadium.

Here, the communicative idea of the building takes on the simplistic vernacular nicknames often applied to iconic projects and uses it as a fuel to fire the design process. This might be read as architecture reaching out to its public through the mechanism of metaphor. Equally, the bleak critique that is offered is the shrinking possibility of architecture as practised by architects: that the facade becomes the remaining site for architectural activity. There is a ruthlessness in FOA's use of communication. A project such as John Lewis in Leicester (2008) operates somewhere between corporate branding and architectural polemic.

FOA, Ravensbourne, London, 2010
above: The use of non-periodic tiling and Gothic rose windows refers to historical archetypes and flower patterns but also symbolises the function of the building as a college for digital media.

FOA, John Lewis Department Store and Cineplex, Leicester, 2008
opposite: The richly patterned layered glass cladding is inspired by the patterned lace that the store is famous for. The cladding is conceived as a veil over the mass of the building.

Terunobu Fujimori

Fujimori's principal form of activity is as a historian of modern Japanese architecture, although even here his methodology can be described as radically Post-Modern. In 1974 he set up the Tokyo Detective Agency whereby he and his associates, armed with cameras and maps, wandered around Tokyo seeking out forgotten or hidden Western-style buildings. This highly idiosyncratic approach to architectural research also informs his practice, which he started at the unusually late age of 44 when he was commissioned to design the Jinchokan Moriya Historical Museum (1991) in his home town, Chino City in Nagano, Japan.

Fujimori's work seems to exist in another domain, somewhere outside of the machinations of contemporary architectural culture. Instead, he produces buildings whose saturation of narrative would place them comfortably as folk illustrations. Their suggestive – and extreme – forms seem to connect Japanese traditions to

the strange pavilions of John Hejduk as though viewed through the eyes of Dr Seuss – a kind of comic-strip exaggeration of a fictitious vernacular that nevertheless exudes authenticity.

Buildings such as the Onsen Spa building in Oita (2006) reject the languages of abstraction in favour of an alternative folk art, featuring trees growing out of roofs and stripey, charred wood cladding. Even stranger is perhaps the Tree tea house, literally a tea house in the trees which would not look out of place on the sets of either *Hansl and Gretl* or *Star Wars*. Oddest and most idiosyncratic of all is his urban proposal for a flooded Tokyo from 2002, which depicted a series of anthill-like towers constructed from wood and coral in order to capture CO_2 emissions. Through these and many other projects, a number of which he has been directly involved in the construction of, Fujimori demonstrates a radically Post-Modern approach to contemporary architecture that is communicative and expressive of social content, while involving itself in a very individual take on the manipulation of familiar form.

Terunobu Fujimori, Lamune Onsen, Oita, Japan, 2006
left: The building is distinguished by its distinctive charred-wood cladding, which gives a strong graphic effect while creating a tactile quality that alludes to traditional Japanese architecture.

Terunobu Fujimori, Tokyo Plan 2101, 2002
right: Model shown at the Venice Bienalle in 2006. The project – a plan for a flooded Japan – was ridiculed as 'fantasy' at the time of the exhibition, but now seems prescient in the light of the Japanese earthquake and tsunami in 2011.

Atelier Bow-Wow's book, *Pet Architecture* (World Photo Press, 2001), which catalogued the unplanned, provisional patchworks of Tokyo buildings through carefully observed architectural drawings, was a kind of manifesto on the ordinary. More specifically, it recognised a particular kind of extraordinary that can be found in the un-designed, extra-architectural urban environments that surround us. This project, the apparent objectivity of which allows us to look at the familiar with a fresh and clear-eyed vision, recognises what architecture might learn from what would normally be regarded as unresolved and un-architectural mutations of the urban environment.

Atelier Bow-Wow's concern with the ordinary remains apparent in its design work. With lightness and humour, Bow-Wow works with what might be described as the contemporary vernacular. Traces that suggest the personality of occupation and elements of ingenious improvisation become part of an architectural language that is driven by a sense of narrative.

Architecture here becomes a way of suggesting stories through material and space, and whose form is derived by the intersection of the narratives of client, context and brief. What might in other hands remain ugly and ordinary are reconfigured as ways for architecture to enter into dialogue with its users and environment.

Atelier Bow-Wow, Double Chimney, Karuizawa, Nagano, Japan, 2008
top: An archetypal house is split and folded open to create an architecture that is somehow both familiar and radically altered.

above: The interior of the house displays distortions of the everyday domestic landscape.

John Körmeling

Prefiguring the ironic communication-based work of recent Dutch product designers, John Körmeling has been engaged in a cross-disciplinary exploration of communication, social context and formal manipulation of the familiar since the early 1980s. He works across the disciplines of sculpture, architecture and urban design, and has an ironic attitude to questions of form and content that is exemplified in projects such as Distribution Centre PTT (fashionable architectural arbitrariness saved by a roof on legs) (Den Bosch, 1984), where, as the name suggests, a piece of gratuitous formalism is 'saved' by being placed under a generic pitched roof structure. His work often gives witty visual expression to infrastructural

and urban design problems, such as in his public space proposal Museumplein (the shortest and widest motorway of the Netherlands; a relief for cars) (Amsterdam, 1988), which is essentially a giant car park offering a wry commentary on the relationship between the car and urban space in our congested cities.

More recent projects have made use of generic architectural typologies that are rendered strange through unexpected location or some other surprising inflection. For example, the Pioneer House (1999) is an Edward Hopper-esque clapboard house that teeters in surreal fashion on top of a three-storey commercial building adjacent to a motorway in Rotterdam. The Rotating House (2008) comprises an archetypal Dutch suburban house which looks odd enough sitting on a traffic island in Tilburg, but whose true weirdness is revealed when one realises that it moves slowly around the perimeter of the island on a 20-hour cycle.

This approach permeates Körmeling's largest project to date, Happy Street, which formed the Dutch Pavilion at the 2010 Shanghai Expo. Happy Street aims to be an archetypal convivial street containing a mix of functions such as a house, a shop, a factory, a farm and a petrol station, and which, according to Körmeling, forms the basis for social life. It is no ordinary street, however, as it takes the form of a gradually rising figure-of-eight ramp raised on piloti off which all of the archetypal buildings are cantilevered. The result is a cross between a surreal fairground ride and an oriental 'floating world'-style painting made real, which manifests Körmeling's ability to use familiar urban elements to create something both heterogeneous and unworldly.

John Körmeling, Pioneer House, Rotterdam, 1999
above: The house is elevated above the roof of the customs house at the container harbour in Rotterdam docks.

John Körmeling, Happy Street, Dutch Pavilion, Shanghai Expo, 2010
opposite top: A surreal cross between a typical street and a fairground ride.

John Körmeling, Rotating House, Tilburg, 2008
opposite bottom: The otherwise normal-looking house moves gradually around the perimeter of the roundabout creating a startling and bizarre roadside experience for passing drivers.

Crimson is an office of architectural historians, a concept that in itself recomposes the relationship of history to practice. History, Crimson seems to say, is not just a chronology of the past, and being a historian is not simply an act of rearranging or refining our understanding of it. Instead, history might be a weapon that can cleave into the present and project into the future.

Described as 'activist academics', Crimson's work is both a critique of postwar planning and a lament for its decline. With a particular interest in postwar new towns, Crimson documents obsessively the ways in which these places have been abandoned by planning but have also gained other unimagined lives through the ways they have been occupied. Through this research the historians explore the relationship of politics to design.

While the research is concerned with understanding these complex and contradictory places, it is through active projects such as WiMBY! in the Rotterdam suburb of Hoogvliet that their unusual form of practice occurs. Here, research, both historical and contemporary, acts as a mechanism for developing propositional projects that engage community groups, developers, architects and designers, planners and politicians into an active dialogue.

Narratives of places and the politics that shape them become a means of constructing potential escape routes from the fate history may consign us to.

Crimson Architectural Historians, WiMBY!, Hoogvliet, Rotterdam, 2001–7
WiMBY! developed and implemented a series of varied projects that ranged from experimental buildings to small-scale interventions in the new town of Hoogvliet. These were informed by a creative analysis of Hoogvliet's past, present and speculative future. The underlying conviction was that the best and most inspiring basis for the future of this postwar town was to enhance, renew and make the best use of Hoogvliet's existing characteristics and qualities, both physical and social.

'Learning from' was a central mode of Post-Modern practice, the gaze of which was fixed on the context that surrounded it rather than on a utopian other. This generated the idea that architectural practice might operate as a way of understanding the complexity of the contemporary city. Its polemic recognised that the city's physical, social and economic characteristics could operate as the site of architectural action.

CUP stands in this tradition, pursuing the idea that the city is an operative system that is simultaneously physical, legal, economic, social and political, and that these are the conditions that inform the nature of its occupation. Here, the idea of learning from the environments around us – and publicly sharing this learning – becomes central to the centre's practice.

As a form of activism and advocacy, the work of CUP and its founder Damon Rich focuses on research, communication and speculation. Education, publication and exhibition become ways of working within the existing networks of the city. This is a form of practice that resites architecture as a practice within specific localities, exploring the relationship of communities to the cities and spaces around them.

These are projects that rethink architecture's possibilities by addressing and working within the systems, laws, policies and other invisible forces that shape our cities.

Damon Rich, Red Lines Housing Crisis Learning Center, St Louis-Boston-New York City-Utrecht-Vienna, 2006–9
top: Rich's Red Lines Housing Crisis Learning Center explored the effects of financial risk on the built environment. Using formats of interview, public engagement, graphics, models, videos and archival materials the project examined the impact of mortgages and loans on homes, housing and communities, how in effect cities are both constructed and destroyed by these ever more complex financial instruments.

Damon Rich/CUP, Subsidized Landscape, 2003–5
above: This research and exhibition project explored the ways in which governments in the US incentivise real-estate development.

Most often involved with projects for public space, muf's central concern is the definition, critique and construction of the idea of publicness, both as a concept and as its physical manifestation.

Characterised by its close relationship with context and users, the firm's projects unpick the social, economic and political narratives of place before reworking these relationships into new configurations. Through an approach of 'close looking', of recognising and cataloguing specific contextual histories and uses, muf draws out the latent potentialities of sites to perform as an active resource for their communities and users.

Narrative is deployed as a device to understand and recognise local histories and significances as well as a mechanism to corral a sometimes disparate range of references, tactics and uses together. Narrative here becomes a form of resistance to the blankness of contemporary public space, a way of engaging with a wider idea of use and of publicness. It also informs the language of the design, which becomes active as a form of communication and experience. muf's often intricate and textural spaces alchemise the political content of its projects into more poetic resolution.

muf, Barking Town Square, London, 2005–8
As part of muf's public realm design of Barking's new town square, this 7-metre (22.9-foot) high folly recreates a fragment of the imaginary lost past of Barking. The project involved a number of diverse groups in its detail design, such as students from the theatre school, elders from the Afro-Carribean lunch club and apprentices from the local bricklayers' college.

Hild und K's project for this facade refurbishment in Berlin-Schöneberg is a case study in architecture as media. Its simple move is to take the photocopied elevation of the original building – the only surviving architectural information – and replay it, building at 1:1. In this way, the faults and errors that the process of photocopying has introduced – the ways in which lines have thickened and thinned, become abstracted, smudged, and blurred and distorted by the mechanism of reproduction – are inscribed architecturally. The suggestion is that architecture is part of this reprographic process, that architecture is a form of media too.

Within a project where historical context and reconstruction are significant, this facade becomes a way of recognising historical concerns but at the same time resisting historical pastiche. Its forms may suggest the stucco facades of 19th-century architecture, but the design process recalls the feedback of the Jesus and Mary Chains guitar's or Andy Warhol's silkscreens.

Here, Hild und K suggests that being modern, being part of the contemporary world, does not mean rejecting history but rather developing a position in relation to it. In fact, developing this nuanced relationship with history is a way of finding out what being modern might actually mean. ⌂

Text © 2011 John Wiley & Sons Ltd. Images: p 47 © FAT; pp 48-9 © John Gollings; p 50 © Meyer Dudesek Architekten; p 51(t) © Valerio Olgiati/Archive Olgiati; p 51(b) © Javier Miguel Verme; p 52 © Benedict Luxmore/arcaidimages.com; p 53 © Foreign Office Architects, photo Peter Jeffree; p 54(l) © Edward Sumner/View Pictures; p 54(r) © Akihisa Masuda; p 55 © Atelier Bow-Wow; pp 56-7 © Peter Cox; p 58 © Crimson Architectural Historians; p 59 © Damon Rich; p 60 © muf architecture/art; p 61 © Michael Heinrich.

Hild und K Architekten, Facade refurbishment in Belzigerstrasse, Berlin-Schöneberg, Berlin, 1999
The building replays its own historical facade in ghost form using the documentary evidence of found drawings as the basis for reconstruction.

CONTEXTUAL COUNTERPOINT

In recent decades, conservationists and planners have co-opted contextualism, reducing it to a tool for enforcing urban conformity. Here **Charles Jencks** reclaims contextualism as a dynamic design strategy. He identifies four different contextual treatments that as well as ensuring continuity are potentially transformative.

Over the last 40 years, the architectural concept of contextualism, borrowed from literature, has missed an important distinction within Post-Modern practice. For many commentators and Prince Charles it has come to mean being in keeping with the surrounding neighbourhood, and thus is used by planning boards to enforce conformity. Why Post-Modernists allowed the co-option of one of their better ideas, and did not protest or explain more clearly what they were about, remains a mystery. But it is time to change that *idée reçue*. They had already designed another strategy beyond mimicking. In 40 years the contextual idea developed into four different strategies underscored by formal tropes. These confirm that Post-Modernists care about the neighbourhood coherence and urban fabric but seek to extend them with transforming continuity, like musical variations on a theme. 'Contextual counterpoint' is thus a hybrid trope borrowed from literature and music to illuminate a moral form of urbanism. ◬

1

Punctuated jazz is an approach deriving from James
Stirling's particular use of collage composition at the Neue
Staatsgalerie in Stuttgart, designed in 1977 and opened in
1984 – the key work of Post-Modern classicism. Vernacular,
modern and historical themes are melded together here as
a contextual infill and are punctuated by counterpointing
incidents in highly coloured High Tech. The irony of using this
style almost always as symbolic ornament was almost never
understood by British commentators, and thus a major lesson
was missed. These High-Tech elements signal the taxi drop-
off point, entrance areas and the main pedestrian routes.
The background styles – neighbourhood vernacular, modern
concrete, banded and arched Neo-Romanesque, coved Neo-
Egyptian, Álvar Aalto, 1920s Stuttgart – are all underplayed
but present. Thus the whole neighbourhood ensemble is
knitted together with high-culture moments, an approach
Aldo Rossi took in a more monumental direction.

2

The variable chameleon. There are several
notable examples of this type, Robert Venturi's
National Gallery Extension, London (1991)
(below), Hans Hollein's Haus House, Vienna
(1990) and Stirling's Clore Gallery, London
(1986). The variable chameleon differs from
the natural animal in taking on different
adjacent codes to mediate them as it undulates
around a large city block. But it transforms
each imitation to send another message, in
the Venturi version creating new 19th-century
'ghost pilasters' to confront the Miesian 'cuts' to
either side. Mediation here is to acknowledge
and respect old, new and the highly used
corner function.

3a

The ad hoc Time City as a palimpsest.
Herzog & de Meuron's Forum La Caixa,
Madrid (2008) takes existing urban
fragments and makes a holistic collage from
them in the vertical dimension. The bottom
of the city is opened up to movement, the
old brick facades are lifted off the ground to
hold the museum, and the top floor imitates
in shape and ornament the morphology and
style of Madrid's past culture, including the
Arabic. Thus preservation is mixed with
paraphrasing, repair and rewriting. Like the
re-minted coins of Rome, these palimpsests
make an enjoyable art of urban time.

3b

The repaired and paraphrased Time City. This is a first cousin of the former category, which often comes out of war damage and the symbolism of rebirth. In Germany, particularly Munich, the approach was first well worked out by Hans Döllgast at the Alte Pinakothek (1957) (top) and then by Josef Wiedemann at the Glyptothek (1980) (bottom). Recently, David Chipperfield has left his Minimalist abstraction for the Post-Modern mixed strategy at the Neues Museum, Berlin (2009). Again it is repairing, reproducing and paraphrasing in new materials the work of time. These multiple methods and materials may then be given a light whitewash to pull them together.

4

Contrapuntal counterpoint. The most risky version of Post-Modernist contextualism is that carried through with brilliance by Edouard François at the Hotel Fouquet, Paris (2006). This pastiche is a sensual amalgam of the legislated tastes of the 8th arrondissement and a hotel that wanted to put as much space into a six-storey typology as they could get away with. You have to look twice at the details, the variations in material and colour to see the point. Precast grey concrete is played smooth, rusticated and rough; and then dark and light. It is carefully woven with metal, glass and concrete into an all-over grammar. An adjacent Haussmann facade set the building code, and then the template for the concrete castings. But while the main facades look five storeys, the overlapping grey picture windows show the truth. These symbolic TV sets indicate the individual hotel rooms. They suggest the reality of eight floors above ground and five below. To signal that you know that François knows that you know that all in Haussmannian Paris is not what it seems, note the way cornice lines are broken, and *oeils-de-boeuf*, at the top, are eroded by the windows. The counterpoint is contrapuntal, the pastiche Mozartian.

VIRTUAL CORPSES, FIGURAL SECTIONS AND RESONANT FIELDS

The 'figural section' is one of the most potent but under used forms of architectural communication. It enables slices, extrusions, fragments and surfaces of buildings to become the media of the non-expressive and deadpan. Here **Sean Griffiths of FAT** looks at Venturi Scott Brown's influence in the development of the figural section and how it has evolved into a key trope in his practice's own work.

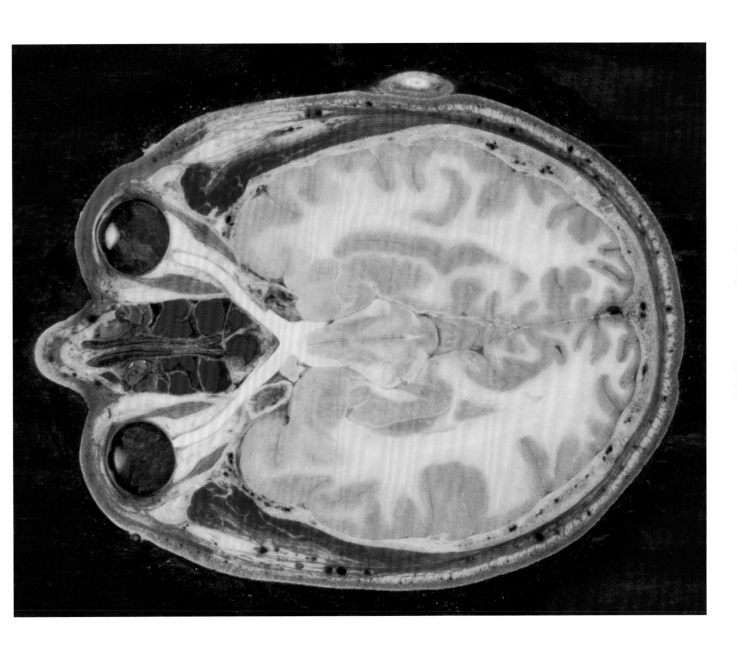

Virtual Corpses

In 1993 following his execution for murder in Texas, Joseph Paul Jernigan was sliced into 1,871 sections, approximately 1-millimetre (0.039 inches) thick. Each slice was photographed in sequence and scanned into a computer. The result was animated to create a virtual journey through the human body.[1]

In this animation, each slice refers to the next one and to the body as a whole. Each is a fragment that stands alone but refers to something else. The slice's power as an artefact comes from its retention of something essentially human, despite its being reduced to a scientific specimen. As such it represents not only itself, but by implication that of which it was once a part: the whole that is now absent.

Despite the inanimate nature of architecture, its relationship to anthropomorphism makes the violence of incisions into built fabric as resonant as those made into human flesh. The artist Gordon Matta-Clark, for example, was famous for his surgical operations on buildings about to be demolished. In works such as *Bingo* (1974) and *Conical Intersect* (Paris, 1975) there is a visceral, corporeal quality to the cuts made into architecture which perhaps exceeds that exhibited by a slice of a murderer's body, whose mutilations are specifically designed to facilitate a particular kind of objective gaze. In a sense the 'coolness' of this neater disfigurement is more chilling than the 'expressive' quality of Matta-Clark's interventions.

The front facade of FAT's Sint Lucas Art Academy in the Netherlands (2006) is a disembodied architectural slice. Like a piece of Jernigan's body, it refers to something absent. Just as the body is a fragment of something human with its humanity removed, the academy's front facade is a fragment of something architectural with the architectural meaning removed. With the human body, the very absence of humanity makes that humanity excessively present, so with Sint Lucas, removal of the authentic architectural meanings (the structural reason for the form, for example) makes the meaning more present.

The Sint Lucas facade is related to death in another way. When buildings die they become ruins. Such fragmented remains are also like slices of body, and the sense of death that pervades a ruin is part of its romantic quality. By contrast there is nothing romantic about the slice of a cadaver, just as there is nothing romantic about the Sint Lucas screen, which looks like a ruin but has more in common with artist Patrick Caulfield's emotionless depiction of ruins than it does with those of, say, Giovanni Battista Piranesi. Both the corpse of Jernigan and the Sint Lucas facade are representations deliberately devoid of emotional content. The former is a disinterested, objective, purely scientific way of seeing of the kind that Michel Foucault refers to in the opening chapter of *The Birth of the Clinic*.[2] The latter is a similarly objective Pop Art way of seeing. Both might be considered examples of the deadpan – a method of depicting meaning with minimal expression.

Early practitioners of Post-Modernist architecture, such as Denise Scott Brown and Robert Venturi, were influenced by the deadpan, objective qualities in the work of Pop artists such as Ed Ruscha and Andy Warhol. They saw the removal of emotional content as a useful device that would help their analyses remain objective or, in their words, 'non-judgemental'. The most potent project of early Post-Modernism was, perhaps, Robert Venturi's 'Bill-ding board' competition entry for the National College Football Hall of Fame, designed in 1967. Here the building was almost secondary to the project's main element – an enormous electronic signboard. Here, again, the emotional qualities of late 1960s Brutalism – expressive materialism and bombastic formalism – is eschewed in favour of a thin surface carrying primitive electronic information.

Gordon Matta-Clark, *Bingo*, 1974
opposite: Building fragments, three sections. Matta-Clark's cuts into buildings are analogous to incisions into the human body and are arguably more visceral and less clinical than scientific operations on the human body, which are carried out under the auspices of an 'objective' gaze.

Patrick Caulfield, *Ruins* (screenprint), 1964
below: In contrast to images of ruins by previous artists such as Piranesi that were full of dramatic lighting effects, Caulfield's rendition is devoid of romanticism and deliberately deadpan.

FAT, Sint Lucas Art Academy, Boxtel, The Netherlands, 2006
bottom: The front facade of Sint Lucas is, in one reading, like a slice of an enormous Gothic cake suggesting a slice analogous to those to which the body of Joseph Paul Jernigan was subjected.

71

The stage-set-like character of the architecture reinforces this theatrical quality. The 'house' image acts as a sign for 'home' and yet its 'home-i-ness' is undermined by a series of distortions.

Figural Sections

The facade at Sint Lucas and the Bill-ding board projects are very different examples of what can be called the 'figural section', defined here as a flattened architectural element taking the form of a slice, extrusion, fragment or surface for information, offering a rich but non-expressive, deadpan or objective form of communication. These qualities counteract the expressionistic spatial promiscuity that characterises much current architecture.

As a surface-based rather than volumetric element, the figural section is vulnerable to the accusation of that most architectural of crimes – being superficial, whereby physical superficiality is conflated with philosophical superficiality. Notwithstanding this facile position, the figural section actually generates a very particular modern spatiality.

At the time of the Bill-ding board project, Venturi, Scott Brown and Steven Izenour were about to undertake the studies that were to become the basis of the book *Learning from Las Vegas*, published in 1972.[3] This publication outraged the architectural establishment by promoting commercial signs and advertising billboards as possibly positive elements within the urban landscape. In doing so, it rejected explicitly the Modernist conception of space as a purely geometric entity contained between physical elements, and instead proposed a communicational field into which information in the form of signs was distributed. These elements charged the spaces between them with an interactive interplay of meanings. In the 1990s this embracing of surfaces as carriers of architectural and other forms of communication seemed a relevant point of departure for a conceptual approach to architecture that would counteract the renewed wilful spatiality that was emerging in architecture at the time.

The figural section is a key trope in FAT's work. It is used as a communicative surface, a facade, or else as a sectional element within a space. In whatever form, it acts upon the spaces in which it is placed, altering them both physically and semiologically. In doing so it remains essentially a surface element, superficial in appearance. This straightforward expression is an implicit critique that refutes the Modernist claim that surfaces are insubstantial and architecturally meaningless. One of the key criticisms of Post-Modernist architecture was that its use of historicist appliqué was always facile, insubstantial and fake. However, this is not necessarily the case.

The Figural Section in the Work of FAT

The Blue House in Hackney, London, completed in 2002, displayed an emphatic early use of the figural section. The building has two facades, one of which is a figural section occurring at the front. This comprises a 'fake' cut-out house applied to the main facade of the building that extends to form the garden fence and also effectively thickens the wall at the front of the street elevation to provide a *poche*-like window seat at the landing of the stair. The movement of people up and down the stair creates a piece of domestic theatre that is visible from the street. The stage-set-like character of the architecture reinforces this theatrical quality. The 'house' image acts as a sign for 'home' and yet its 'home-i-ness' is undermined by a series of distortions. A chimney and a bush form part of the image, but are also represented negatively as absences to emphasise the 'cookie cutter' quality of the facade. Odd window sizes distort the sense of perspective, creating a sense of the uncanny in relation to this typical symbol of comfort. The cut-out house is underscaled in relation to both the surrounding buildings and the side elevation of the house, giving a sense of dislocation in relation to the spaces of the street and the internal spaces of the house. It is, for example, difficult to ascertain the positions or numbers of the floors when viewing the building from the outside.

The idea of the non-neutrality of space was explored in a number of domestic interiors that incorporated the *figural section* as the main architectural intervention.

This is exacerbated by the house motif being placed against what appears to be a miniature office building, whose three rows of windows actually denote a single storey. The combination of these elements announces, in a deadpan manner, a house with an office in it. Dislocations of scale are created in relation to both the exterior and interior. The building reconstitutes urban life as a piece of theatre, touching on the dichotomy between reality and representation. In order to leave no one in any doubt about its aspiration to be understood as serious architecture, this false facade follows the tradition of Palladio by being placed in relation to a complex and nuanced architectural plan. It is Adolf Loos on the inside and South Park on the outside.

Resonant Fields

And yet the figural section aims at a different type of spatiality from that of the architectural plan. Going further than Venturi et al, the figural section is part of a communicational field – something like a Deleuzian territory rather than an architectural enclosure.[4] In FAT's early projects, constructions of architectural spaces via the use of physical elements were rejected in favour of the creation of fluid territories, which made use of what might be called 'parasitic architecture' – existing structures appropriated for new uses. The 1993 project Adsite was an exhibition of 200 artworks in bus shelter advertising sites spread across London. It constituted the creation of a territory in two senses: on the one hand, a 'de-territorialised' art gallery distributed itself through the city; on the other hand, a powerful commercial site of communication, usually only available to large corporations, was temporarily 'captured' for different ends. This was the precursor to a number of projects, incorporating devices such as business cards and shopping bags as vehicles for the display and exchange of art. These distributed themselves through the city as fields in a manner opposed to the traditionally enclosed, pure architectural space of the art gallery.

In these projects, the point of interaction between the city occupant and the work is not architectural space but the communicative surface. The art is placed in front of an audience going about their daily business and not actively seeking out art as a gallery visitor would. Art becomes part of a disinterested backdrop in the city, mimicking the role that architecture usually plays. The projects occurred as the Internet made thin surfaces as mediators of complex and changing information part of everyday life. They formed part of a London scene, driven by new tendencies in art, fashion, music, magazines and publishing. Like the Independent Group in the 1950s,[5] FAT (originally conceived as a magazine) was more interested in these phenomena than it was in the architecture of the time. Alongside its urban art projects, it began to explore the possibilities of surface communication in architectural spaces.

Internal Urbanisms

The Leisure Lounge nightclub in London, designed in 1994, featured as its main architectural element an enormous projection screen carrying an ever-changing display, allowing the architectural qualities of the space to respond to the music in an aural extension of Venturi's Bill-ding board concept. The Kistner House, also designed in 1994, drew on the artist Dan Graham's studies of the social and psychological effects of reflection and transparency, and featured another surface-based architectural element. In this case, a bedroom and a bathroom were separated by a one-way mirrored screen whose levels of transparency and reflectivity changed in response to both natural and artificial light conditions. This created a surface within the room whose ambiguous characteristics become articulated via a functionality that veers between privacy, voyeurism and narcissism. In both of these cases, however, the changing nature of a screen's surface conveys both architectural

FAT, Kistner House, Brixton, London, 1996
opposite: View of the bedroom/bathroom.
A one-way mirror screen provides a
communication surface that changes
under different lighting conditions, in this
instance articulating degrees of privacy
and voyeurism.

FAT, Leisure Lounge nightclub,
Holborn, London, 1994
below: View of the main dance hall,
dominated by the main architectural element,
a 15-metre (49.2-foot) projection screen.

FAT, Adsite exhibition of art in bus
shelters, London, 1993
bottom: Adsite used bus shelters to exhibit
200 artworks across London, converting
them into a dispersed gallery and asserting
the power of the two-dimensional surface
as an urban element.

and sociological meanings with the context of a space that was
determined by the nature of its occupation, firmly rejecting the
idea that architectural space is neutral and abstract.

The idea of the non-neutrality of space was explored
in a number of domestic interiors that incorporated the
figural section as the main architectural intervention. In north
London, a former chapel was converted and partitioned by
the facade of a huge shed. There is a clear ambiguity between
the domestic scale of the shed as an object and its 'public' scale
within the interior. This is articulated by the 'advent calendar'-
style windows which, when closed, reinforce the idea of a giant
shed, but when open suggest a public scale facade.

Another house conversion, in south London, features a
figural section of a very different character. A top-lit lateral
extension containing a library makes the rear part of the
house the full width of the plot. The former external wall
becomes part of the interior and is remodelled into a screen
incorporating large, classically detailed openings looking on
to the double-height living room. The effect is of a slice of a
grand Palladian villa squeezed into a modest Victorian terrace
for which it is too small. This play on 'public' and 'private'
scales is further emphasised by the use of overscaled skirting,
architraves and mouldings and by the careful interplay of real
openings and mirrors to create the illusion of other rooms
beyond the modest space of the existing house.

Exterior Urbanisms

At Islington Square, a social housing project in Manchester
(2006), the figural section forms a facade that is violently
dislocated from the building by an abrupt change of
materials and formal language. The exuberantly shaped and
extravagantly patterned brick facade is like a giant slice of
cake wrapping a simple white Modernist box, giving voice to
a series of typological ambiguities. The scheme is a series of

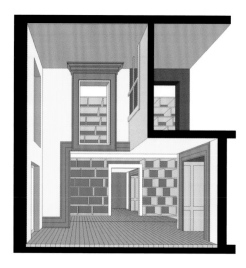

terraces and yet the facade is used to create the illusion of semi-detached villas. Each house is articulated individually by having a different top; however this individuality is undercut by the overscaled brickwork patterns that suggest, but are not true to, the boundaries of each house. The brickwork patterns also reinforce the sense of the facade as a continuous enclosing wall, creating a citadel-like expression of community in opposition to the individual expression of each house. The facades give a clear urban frontage, becoming part of a clearly defined public realm and yet emphatically detach an exclusive world of private alleyways and gardens allowing for the creation of complex spaces of social interaction within the block. By giving grandeur to these modest houses, designed for the local working-class community, the facade also creates a transition of scale in both architectural and social terms.

In contrast, at the Sint Lucas Academy, the facade is physically separated from the buildings that it wraps. This is a 'pure' facade, which like an element in a John Hejduk house,[6] has only one function – to create a public face that communicates the nature of the institution that it represents. It is a concrete billboard, albeit one whose meaning is more ambiguous than the average advertising billboard. But it also represents a clear distinction between architecture and building perhaps appropriate for the way buildings are made today. For, borrowing Pevsner's terminology, the Sint Lucas facade is the 'Lincoln Cathedral' and the ordinary existing buildings it shields the 'bicycle sheds.[7] It allows a relatively modest building to have architectural expression in an age that allows for the construction of buildings, but increasingly, on the grounds of cost, excludes the possibility of architecture. The Sint Lucas screen therefore represents a piece of autonomous architecture devoid of programme and only related to the buildings behind it in the loosest way possible.

'Mere' Facadism

The figural section is a deadpan or objective mode of architectural expression most closely associated with Pop Art. But it is also related to other 'objective' ways of seeing, such as the medical gaze that removes the emotional content from acts of cutting, slicing and dismembering. It allows for expression without the hysterics that characterise today's overexpressive architectural anthems. With the figural section, emotion is experienced as absence. It is cool. One might say it depicts the absence of emotion while at the same time presenting the loss of emotion as a kind of tragedy. Just as Andy Warhol's paintings are more powerful because they avoid the excess of signifying emotion in Abstract Expressionist paintings, so the figural section makes architectural expression more powerful and yet more nuanced. Absence is power.

But for the absence to be felt, abstraction is not enough, hence the section must be figural. It must be representational, so it can depict the absence, the missing 'space', the lack of volume, the loss of depth. It offers only a fragment. The viewer can fill in the gaps.

Facadism is deemed an insult in architecture. An open adoption of it is, on the one hand, a polemical position, designed to expose the conceits of an architectural profession currently in thrall to pornographic spatial excess. On the other hand, the reinvigoration of the facade as a communicative element of architecture is nothing more than the recovery of a long-standing tradition. What's good enough for Palladio is good enough for us. FAT's use of the figural section, far from being a reductive element in architecture, reveals it to be an architectural device which, through plays on scale, function, decoration and symbolism has the ability to create rich ambiguities of social, spatial and architectural meaning, allowing narratives to unfold and enrich the reductive geometrical spaces inherited from our forebears. Not least, in the face of endless worthy architecture and ineffable flights of spatial fantasy, it gives architecture an opportunity to be complex, intricate and relevant. ⚏

Notes

1. Jernigan donated his body to the Visible Human Project, run by the US National Library of Medicine. The project is exhibited at the National Museum of Health and Medicine in Washington DC.
2. In the introduction to *The Birth of the Clinic*, 1963, Foucault compares the description of a mid 18th-century medical examination, full of fantastical visceral detail, with a mid 19th-century description characterised by its 'scientific' language and disinterested gaze informed by the acquisition of objective knowledge. Michel Foucault, *The Birth of the Clinic*, Routledge (Abingdon), 1989, pp ix–x.
3. Robert Venturi, Denise Scott Brown and Steven Izenour, *Learning from Las Vegas*, MIT Press (Cambridge, MA), 1972.
4. This idea of communication 'field' is related to but different in character to the idea of 'field' found, for example, in the writings of Patrik Schumacher and other parametricists as it refers to real-life perceptible fields of objects that communicate directly with each other, as opposed to more abstract, less tangible phenomena derived from modern physics. See Patrik Schumacher, *The Autopoiesis of Architecture*, John Wiley & Sons (London), 2011. For a discussion of Deleuzian territories, see Treatise on Nomadology as published in Gilles Deleuze and Félix Guattari, *A Thousand Plateaus*, trans Brian Massumi. Continuum (London and New York), 2004.
5. The Independent Group was a collection of writers, thinkers, artists and architects who met in London between 1952 and 1955. They are now historically seen as the fathers of Pop Art. They were known for their interest in the paraphernalia of the emerging consumer culture of the 1950s. Key members included Reyner Banham, Alison and Peter Smithson, Richard Hamilton, Eduardo Paolozzi, Nigel Henderson, Lawrence Alloway and John McHale.
6. For example, the Bye House, constructed posthumously in Groningen in the Netherlands, is designed under the auspices of an extreme functionalism, so that each space has only one primary function.
7. 'A bicycle shed is a building; Lincoln Cathedral is a piece of architecture. Nearly everything that encloses space on a scale sufficient for a human being to move in is a building; the term architecture applies only to buildings designed with a view to aesthetic appeal.' Nikolaus Pevsner, *An Outline of European Architecture*, Penguin Books (Harmondsworth), [1942] 1957, p 23.

FAT PROJECTS
MANIFESTING RADICAL POST-MODERNISM

Sean Griffiths, Charles Holland and Sam Jacob of FAT explain how they have developed their own brand of fit-for-purpose Radical Post-Modernism that enables them to actively engage with the specifics of any building project. They work at a diverse range of scales and programmes from art pavilions to social housing and public buildings. Not afraid to magnify the ordinary and the familiar, FAT tackle the often-thorny questions of taste and meaning head on with a joyful verve.

FAT's projects are both critically and socially engaged with their circumstances. The office's interests in architecture and communication, the politics of taste, the relationship of figuration and abstraction are active as architectural mechanisms that are used to engage with the particularities of the brief, context and situation of a project. Rather than simply rhetorically illustrating a position, these approaches bring a wider framework to bear that extends architecture's role from the formal to one that explores the application of critical and cultural agendas.

Through the formation of unholy alliances and strange bedfellows, the projects probe the role of architecture and design in contemporary culture – what it might do for us, what it might represent, and how it might articulate the conditions that surround it.

The projects often employ tactics that seek to amplify architecture's social and cultural content. Copying, appropriation, collage, juxtaposition and rescaling are used to develop narratives of image, materiality and space. These narratives, written explicitly and directly, draw on the specifics of a project's context to develop an architecture that is both extraordinary and familiar.

Grote Koppel, Amersfoort, The Netherlands, 2010

Grote Koppel is a contemporary three-storey palazzo situated adjacent to the Koppelpoort – a historic watergate set within the medieval walls of the old city of Amersfoort. It forms a contextual counterpoint to this structure and sits at the heart of a network of infrastructure comprising the River Eem, a main-line railway and a row of converted 19th-century warehouses that sit on the riverside. The building, containing a restaurant and an office, was commissioned by the developer to commemorate the city's 750th anniversary. It contains an elegant precast-concrete staircase that makes a theatrical contribution to the restaurant spaces, but in essence its main elements are the external facades that enclose a generic in-situ concrete frame. The elevations are conceived as a series of overscaled classical window surrounds that have grown to such an extent that they become the wall. The surrounds are subjected to distortions that create a rippling effect, as if the building were representing its own reflection in water. This effect is further intensified by the fact that the building is indeed reflected in the river. The sense of movement in the facade is also a response to the idea of the building

being viewed from a train on the railway line that flanks the site.

Grote Koppel has a mythical quality. In contrast to the whiteness of the first two floors, the top floor is black, as if it has been burnt out. A sense of potential collapse is also communicated by the diagonal struts that appear in a number of windows, suggesting a building under construction or one in immediate danger of catastrophic collapse.

All of these effects – historical allusion, formal fluidity, narrative suggestion and sense of (de)construction – are undercut by the building's true method of construction. The precast-concrete sandwich panels that make up the walls are generally associated with a uniformity of elements rather than with the variety found here. The jointing of the panels that communicate vertical rhythms is contradicted by the horizontal fluidity of the floor demarcations. An impression of precariousness and haphazard construction is countered by the modernity and solidity of the construction technique.

Despite the simplicity of its programme, Grote Koppel extracts the maximum from its complex and contradictory facades.

Grote Koppel, Amersfoort, The Netherlands, 2010
The building sits in a complex context, fronting on to the River Eem and completing a row of 19th-century warehouses. Beyond the railway line, the roof of the ancient Koppelpoort, a gateway into the walled city, is visible.

Writer's House, Clapham, London, 1998

This conversion of a typical London terraced house creates a complex architectural promenade that weaves through the building. Constructed in 1998, it is the first example in FAT's work of the overt use of classical detailing, which constituted a radical move at the time. This is mainly evident on a figural section separating the main living/entertaining room from a two-storey library that occupies a new lateral extension to the house. Influenced by the lighting effects found in the work of Sir John Soane, the figural section is backlit from a roof light that extends the length of the library.

However, this is no exercise in polite classical expression. The architraves and window surrounds, together with the truncated panelling of the doors, strike a discordant note. This quality is further emphasised by the use of mirrored skirting, doors and wall panels, which create the illusion of further non-existent spaces beyond the room and undermine the stability of the composition.

Scale distortion is major theme in this design, both in relation to the figural section element and the sizes of the skirting and architraves. The effect is one of a large fragment of a grand Palladian house having been squeezed into a small domestic space. The sense of compression is further emphasised by the presence of a writer's study, whose truncated window crashes into the classical element. Through this window it is possible to see a doorway that mirrors the classical opening at first-floor level, further enhancing the sense of ambiguity between real and reflected spaces.

The spaces are heavily layered, so that it is possible to view the garden at the back of the house from the bedroom at the front through a suite of rooms. A rooftop study, in contrast, gives an unobstructed view of the London skyline.

Writer's House, Clapham, London, 1998
View of the living room. A complex layered space of crashing juxtapositions, ambiguities of scale and illusion of space is illuminated via Soanesque backlighting.

The Blue House, Hackney, London, 2002

The Blue House is situated on a tight urban site in Hackney, east London, and contains a family house, an office and a small apartment. Clad in baby-blue clapboard, it combines popular and high-cultural references which are communicated via a cartoonish exterior. This contrasts with a sophisticated interior based on a complex plan influenced by Adolf Loos. The signature elements of the house are two communicative facades or figural sections. The first, situated at the front elevation, comprises an underscaled house motif rendered as a cut-out billboard. This sits in front of the main facade, whose windows give the impression of an underscaled office building, thus communicating in a deadpan fashion the function of the building. The second figural section forms the flank elevation facing the main road and contains overscaled windows, shimmering decorative panels and a cut-out gable undercutting its otherwise Modernist characteristics. These dislocations of scale give the building a highly ambiguous quality that mediates on the relationships between the fake and the real, and the scales of houses and apartment buildings.

These ambiguities are also played out inside the house, where the spaces are free-flowing in a Modernist way but have the character of rooms. Traditional details such as architraves are used to articulate structural elements as both columns and walls, but not quite either. Architraves and door panels also create ambiguities of scale. Doors seem too big for their openings, and architraves too big or too small for the openings they surround. The main stair of the house curves around one of the bedrooms, which is suspended within the main space giving the impression of a building within a building. The stair has a domestic scale when experienced inside the house, but has something of the compressed grandeur of the stair at Derbyshire's Elizabethan Hardwick Hall when viewed from the outside.

The Blue House, Hackney, London, 2002
Front elevation showing house and office motifs incorporating distortions of window sizes and elements picked out negatively and positively.

View showing main facades in ambiguous scale relationships, including underscaled house and office motifs to the street and overscaled side elevation.

Ambiguities of scale are applied throughout the house, including the treatment of panelled doors, skirting and architraves.

'You Make Me Feel Mighty Real', Belsay Hall, Northumberland, 2000

The design of this pavilion, sited in the grounds of a country house, is a copy of a Romanesque church taken from a drawing in a book of anonymous architectural drawings. It is a copy of a copy. This chimes with the history of the site, which consists of a Doric country house designed 'incorrectly' by an amateur architectural enthusiast, set within an apparently natural environment that is in fact a manmade landscape formed within the quarry from which the stone for the house was hewn. This narrative of artificial against natural and amateur fake against professional authenticity informs the design of the pavilion.

Mimicking the architecture of Belsay Hall, the pavilion is an incorrect and underscaled copy of the Romanesque church. The surface of the building is clad in circular metal discs that depict Romanesque details that dissolve into a pixellated 'Magritte' sky on the tower. The discs move and catch the light in the wind, creating a magical effect of rippling light across the surface of the pavilion. Unlike the fake naturalism of the context, this 'Las Vegas' aesthetic is deliberately artificial in character and yet is designed to amplify and respond to the natural characteristics of light and wind while simultaneously creating a counterpoint to the surrounding greenery.

Within the pavilion are two seats from which it is possible to contemplate the forest beyond.

'You Make Me Feel Mighty Real',
Belsay Hall, Northumberland, 2000
A miniature Romanesque church forms a shimmering place of contemplation within the apparently natural, but actually manmade landscape of Belsay Hall.

Sint Lucas Art Academy, Boxtel, The Netherlands, 2006

Sint Lucas is a Dutch art academy situated in the town of Boxtel, near Eindhoven. The project comprises the remodelling of the existing 1950s and 1960s buildings into a more coherent campus containing public spaces, car parking and a garden around which the buildings are arranged. The most visible elements of the school's transformation are a series of concrete screens that articulate the external spaces and respond to the context of the town and the history of the school. These create a new identity for the institution, communicating its status as an institution for creative learning.

The screens are draped like ruins around the existing buildings and respond to, and communicate about, the particularities of the town's urban character and the functions of different parts of the campus. Perhaps most striking is an extruded Gothic screen that looks on to a piazza, wrapping the disparate buildings to create a cohesive frontage. Its style references a nearby castle, the gabled buildings of the town, the architecture of collegiate buildings, and the history of the academy as a monastic painting school, as well as alluding to ruins. Its rendering as a 'Pop' element, devoid of Romanticism, also chimes with the 'Gothic' fashions of the students who inhabit the school. The second 'Pop Gothic' screen separates the piazza and a semi-private garden, maintaining the collegiate/monastic narrative.

A Rationalist-style colonnade fronts the administration block at the other end of the campus, and wraps around – temporarily collapsing to form 'ruined' seating in a nod to James Stirling – to form a canopy in front of the dining hall. The character of this element, together with a vibrant wall pattern, creates the impression of an administrative building fronting a factory. This is in keeping with the suburban nature of the site at this end of the campus. This 'commercial' look also reflects the school's strong contacts with the commercial world. The wall patterns are also derived from religious sources, but are scaled up to create a commercial appearance, thus symbolising the school's history as a religious institution and its present-day relationship to the commercial world.

Sint Lucas Art Academy, Boxtel, The Netherlands, 2006
The 'Pop Gothic' precast-concrete screen creates a new front for the school, gathering the disparate 1960s buildings to create a holistic image.

The screens change in character at the eastern end of the site where the context is more suburban.

View of the new public foyer.

KesselsKramer offices, Amsterdam, 1998

This much-fêted and imitated interior houses an advertising agency inside a 19th-century Gothic church. It is an exercise in contextual counterpoint, and juxtaposes a number of practical yet ambiguous objects and interventions against the existing Gothic architecture. The elements read as either miniature buildings or as large pieces of furniture. This reflects the fact that the church is a registered monument and changes to the fabric of the existing building are prohibited.

The character and scale of the interventions contrast vividly with those of the church. A wooden fort with a tower makes full use of the height of the nave space, providing a mezzanine level for workstations. An elongated lifeguard's tower

provides a showreel room. Other elements include a library in a truncated overscaled shed, fragments of AstroTurf with football pitch markings, and stripy tables creating the workstations. The meeting room is decked out like a sinister fairytale forest.

The overall effect is like a miniature hill-town encased within the church. Its aesthetic draws on everything from folktales to Surrealism to the work of Gordon Matta-Clark. It is a provisional architecture, the opposite of a pristine 'well-designed' office environment. It accommodates the mess and chaos of a creative workplace while retaining a strong sense of the company's identity, which is powerfully communicated to all visitors.

KesselsKramer offices, Amsterdam, 1998
A range of mini buildings and furniture elements at multiple scales form a mini urbanism within the confines of a 19th-century Gothic church.

Islington Square, New Islington, Manchester, 2006

Islington Square is a development of 23 new houses for social rent in Manchester. The development is part of a wider regeneration project called New Islington, and rehouses the residents of an existing council estate built in the 1970s.

The new houses were designed by FAT through consultation with the residents, exploring and giving expression to their tastes and lifestyles. The conflicting demands of the brief – the residents' preference for 'traditional' typologies of housing and the developer's desire for 'world-class, contemporary' architecture – led to the development of a hybrid form combining the suburban semi-detached house with the urban terrace.

As part of the design process, the DIY alterations to the residents' existing houses were photographed. These interiors became the inspiration for the design process. The new houses develop these themes of DIY adaption into a public language that articulates the tastes of the residents within the context of the masterplan. The overscaled facade plays a key role in communicating these complex and contradictory tensions. The profile of this element and the ornamental objects attached to it give spatial and symbolic expression to the individual houses behind. At the same time, the superscaled brick decoration relates to the urban context as a whole.

Behind the facade, the houses have an L-shaped plan that allows for degrees of flexibility in how they are laid out. The plan gives each major room a double aspect that, combined with the generous floor-to-ceiling heights, brings large amounts of natural light into the interiors.

At the front of the house is a small courtyard space protected by the facade, which can be used for parking or as a garden. At the rear is a larger, private garden space that links to a 'ginnel', a shared space for all the residents.

Islington Square, New Islington, Manchester, 2006
top: Each individual house is defined by its own gable, the shape of which helps create aesthetic tension by truncating the massive brickwork patterning. The visual strength of the facade comfortably accommodates residents' additions, such as satellite dishes.

above left: View of row of two-storey houses showing the use of polychromatic brick patterns and differentiated gables denoting individual houses, paired as in semi-detached houses but forming a unified terrace.

above right: Detail of three-storey block. The brick facade is a figural section with houses behind. There is an abrupt aesthetic change between the brick facade and the white-rendered Modernist boxes behind it that contain the houses.

Thornton Heath Library, Thornton Heath, London, 2010

This project included the modernisation and extension of an existing Edwardian library constructed in 1914. The major external intervention is the creation of a pavilion that provides a new entrance sequence and a public reading room. The form of this pavilion is both a counterpoint and a continuation of the classical language of the existing building.

The pavilion is formed from polished precast concrete that relates tonally to the library's Portland stone dressing. Monumental lettering adorns the top and spells out the building's function within the context of a high street full of temporary commercial signs. The pavilion thus acts both as an explicit piece of communication and a new, functioning space; it is an inhabited sign. The design conflates civic, heraldic and commercial imagery to make a new pubic language.

Thornton Heath Library, Thornton Heath, London, 2010
top: View of the library from the street showing the relationship between the existing library and the new front extension incorporating a new entrance, access and reading room. The addition is a contemporary response to the heraldic symbolism of the old entrance to the existing building.

above left: The entrance ramp faces a new glazed reading room. Conceived as a community living room, the reading room creates a transparent connection with the street.

above centre: The reading room projects out to the street, signifying a more open relationship to the context.

The Villa, Hoogvliet, The Netherlands, 2008

The Villa forms the centrepiece of the Heerlijkheid park designed by FAT on the outskirts of Rotterdam. It functions as a community and arts centre and was commissioned to provide a new civic focus for the Dutch new town of Hoogvliet. Typologically, the Villa attempts to marry the generic light industrial shed, a ubiquitous feature of the highway-edge landscape the park occupies, with an architecture that is expressive, communicative and entirely specific to Hoogvliet's own circumstance.

The park in which the Villa is sited is a suburban tribute to the allegorical landscapes of the grand country houses. It comprises bridges, seats and water features arranged both formally and in nature. Its follies are 'hobby-huts' for the use of the local community, its bridges are billboard-like exclamations of civic pride, and its sculptures are BBQ pits, pink picnic tables and basket-woven houses perpetually reconstructed by schoolchildren – ruins in reverse.

The new-town narrative of the bucolic versus the urban and its attendant suburban activities is carried over into the design of the Villa. Essentially a simple industrial shed, the building is clad in a figurative timber rain-screen which, like a cartoon strip, tells the story of Hoogvliet as it moves round the building. Above the entrance, a series of up-stands depicts the pipes and chimneys of the oil refinery, visible beyond the park, which gave the town its *raison d'être*. As it progresses, the screen picks out the saw-tooth rooftops of local industrial buildings, the stanchions of agricultural sheds and tree canopies which represent the bucolic dream of the town's distant memory. In doing so it makes reference to the specificity of Hoogvliet's history and the generic history of new towns as places that attempted to combine the best of the town and the country. The building's image-narrative develops these references into an explicit visual story that projects an image that operates as a potential collective future – a kind of 'Punk-Pop' contemporary civic architecture.

The most striking feature of the Villa is its main entrance, an extreme figurative representation of a golden forest glade that morphs into a bench. Beyond this is a piano nobile containing a grand stair ironically rendered in municipal style. The interior of the villa is shed-like, a quality emphasised and undercut by the bright pink steel structure. Standard industrial windows give views out on to the park, but are framed by the figurative details of the rain-screen.

Appropriately for a building designed in close consultation with the multicultural community, and in fulfilling its programmatic ambition to act as what the Constructivists termed a 'social condenser', the building hosts events ranging from weddings, circumcision parties, dance nights and vegetable-growing competitions to educational events for both schoolchildren and PhD programmes.

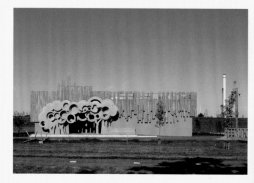

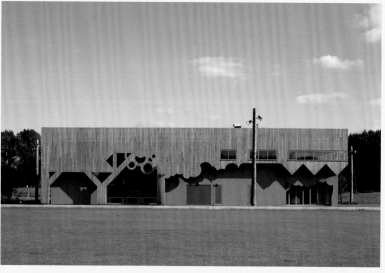

The Villa, Hoogvliet, The Netherlands, 2008
Front view. A cartoon strip rain-screen riffs on the iconography of the local oil refinery (visible in the background) and is surmounted by a 'Punk-Pop' depiction of a forest glade which marks the main entrance.

Rear view. As the rain-screen continues around the building, it picks out the details of agricultural barns, abstracted tree canopies and the saw-tooth roofs of industrial sheds with a small nod to Le Corbusier's Villa Savoye.

The Villa sits within the Heerlijkheid park, designed by FAT, the programme of which is determined by the hobbies and activities of the local community. In the original park concept, these are displayed across the landscape to create an Archigram-esque suburban pleasure garden.

Nonument, Scheveningen, The Hague, 2002

Commissioned by the City of The Hague and the Stroom art organisation as a surveillance hut for a bicycle park, this little building also acts as a piece of public theatre. It is sited on the edge of the seaside resort of Scheveningen at the end of a long promenade of restaurants, bars and shops. The design of the hut responds to this landscape of bright lights, big signs and theatrical seaside architecture. It also refers to other more ambiguous forms including monuments, fortifications and lighthouses.

A steeply sided object like a tiny, truncated hill contains the security hut and storage for cycle equipment. On top of the hill is a model of a typical Dutch house that appears to periodically catch fire. Every half an hour, neon lights inside the house flicker and a smoke machine emits bursts of steam.

The Nonument has become a popular landmark in the Netherlands and was featured on a national Dutch stamp. ᗄ

FAT, Fiets & Stal, 2005. Scheveningen

Ne der land €0,69

PRIORITY

Text © 2011 John Wiley & Sons Ltd. Images: pp 80, 81(t) © Jeroen Musch; pp 81(b), 83(b), 85(tr), 89(t), 89(bl) © FAT; p 82 © Adrian Taylor; p 83(t) © Morley von Sternberg; pp 84(l), 85(tl) © Dennis Gilbert/View Pictures; p 84(r) © Frans Barten; p 85(b), 89(br) courtesy FAT; p 86(t) © Len Grant; p 86(bl) © James White; p 86(br) © Timothy Soar; p 87 © Paul Riddle, paul-riddle. com; p 88 © Photography Rob Parrish

Nonument, Scheveningen, The Hague, 2002
A small house on a mini monumental hill catches fire periodically. The building responds to the nearby war memorial in a manner that also acknowledges the seaside architecture of the local context.

Conceived as a piece of built communication, the building succeeded in capturing the affections of the Dutch nation, to the extent that its image became a piece of communication in the form of a stamp.

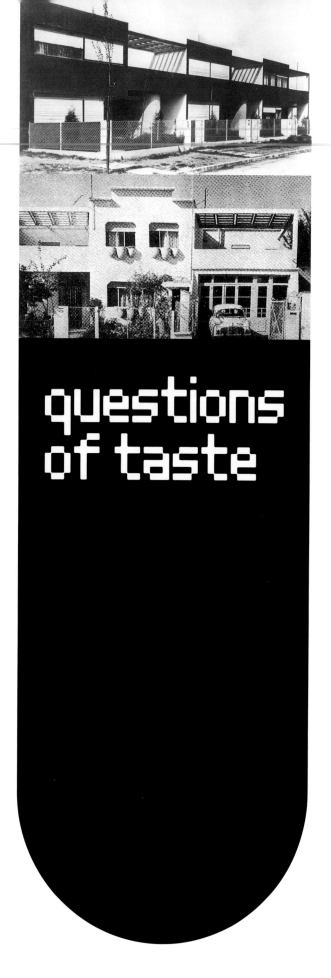

questions of taste

Charles Holland of FAT picks up the Post-Modern baton from Venturi Scott Brown and Charles Jencks and raises the neglected topic of taste. Though the way architecture is experienced by people is bound up with taste, it remains an area of discomfort for architects – tied up with awkward discussions of privilege and class. Holland shows how in FAT's Islington Square housing project the DIY taste of the residents was not only embraced, but fully accommodated.

Consumption … is devious, it is dispersed, but it
insinuates itself everywhere, silently and invisibly,
because it does not manifest itself through its own
products but rather through its ways of using products
imposed by a dominant economic order.
— Michel de Certeau, *The Practice of Everyday Life*,
1984, pp xii–xiii[1]

Charles Jencks' 1977 book *The Language of Post-Modern
Architecture*[2] features two very different photographs of the
houses Le Corbusier designed at Pessac, France, in 1928. One
was taken shortly after their completion and the other some 40
years later. In the second picture the houses have been radically
altered. Residents' modifications have transformed the stark,
sculptural beauty of the original houses and defiled them with
DIY clutter. Flower baskets hang from the facades, ribbon
windows have been replaced with traditional ones and small
extensions have grown up around the edges.

Here we see what happens to architecture once the
architect has walked away. Not as a lament (in the case of
famous buildings lost through demolition) but as part of the
order of things. It is extremely rare for the life of a building
after its completion to be included within architectural
history. Buildings tend to be represented at the moment of
their completion, before the effects of weather, degradation,
adaptation or use take effect. So, the question the images pose
is this: has the architecture been ruined by insensitive abuse or
have the houses merely been adapted to better suit their use? Or
to put it another way, have the artistic ambitions of the architect
been overwritten by the everyday requirements of the residents?

Lurking within *The Language of Post-Modern Architecture*
is the suggestion of another, alternative version of architectural
history: self-build, DIY, squats and various forms of temporary
settlement take up a surprisingly large chunk of the book. It is
one of the few times in mainstream architectural theory when
the significance of the architect as sole author has been called
into question. Certainly, subsequent 'isms' – deconstructivist,
late modern or parametric – have aspired towards the grand
project or the significant icon, and have been predicated on the
absolute supremacy of the architect's vision. Of all the forms
of 'outsider' architecture included in Jencks' book, though, it
is the do-it-yourself additions at Pessac that are perhaps the
most provocative. While the activities of the 1960s counterculture directly informed the avant-garde, the more prosaic
world of do-it-yourself has been largely ignored by architectural
theory. One of the reasons for this is that it is the product of a
social group – working and lower-middle-class families – that
have otherwise played only a passive role in the history of
architecture.

Such people do play a central role in Michel de Certeau's
book *The Practice of Everyday Life* though. In the introduction
to this seminal study, de Certeau states that: 'The investigation
of everyday practices was first delimited negatively by the
necessity of not locating cultural difference in groups associated
with the counter culture – groups that were already singled out,
often privileged, and already partly absorbed into folklore.'[3]

De Certeau's study looked at how, contrary to popular
prejudice, everyday practices such as cooking, walking and
watching television involved an active and creative degree of
participation. De Certeau avoided looking at predictable sites of
resistance to the dominant culture in order to concentrate on the
radical possibilities of everyday life. Similarly, in architecture,
while issues of temporality and prefabrication have been
absorbed into the official discourse along with the radical-chic
of the 1960s counterculture, subtler instances of unofficial
architecture such as owner adaptation have not.

The inclusion of the photographs of Pessac in Jencks'
book was not neutral or innocent, however. They were used as
witnesses for the prosecution, evidence of Modernism's perceived
failings. Endorsing this point is not the purpose here though. It
would be a mistake to interpret DIY as some kind of spontaneous
expression of popular desire. After all, popular taste is as
circumscribed and ideological as elite taste. If the modifications at
Pessac are important, it is not as an alternative to Modernism, but
as a successful outcome of it. Instead of being used as a precursor
to yet another style, the photographs in *The Language of Post-
Modern Architecture* can be seen as suggesting an alternative view
of who the authors of architecture really are.

The potential of this strain of thought was effectively cut off by Post-Modernism's subsequent conflation with big business, crass commercialism and the abandonment – rather than continuation – of the Modernist project. It remains a potentially radical legacy, one yet to be fully mined. To explore this claim it is worth going back a bit to pick up the thread.

Post-Modernism: An Incomplete Project

One of the more unlikely champions of early Post-Modern architecture was the American artist Dan Graham. Graham wrote a series of essays addressing the work of Robert Venturi and Denise Scott Brown, which are collected together in his 1993 book *Rock My Religion*.[4] Venturi and Scott Brown repaid the compliment, citing Graham's 1966 photo essay *Homes for America* as an important influence on their own research into the architecture of 'the everyday'.

This mutually admiring relationship might seem perplexing, especially to British critics used to mauling Venturi and Scott Brown for their unwarranted association with Prince Charles via the Sainsbury Wing debacle. But Venturi and Scott Brown's interest in popular taste and in the genealogy of suburban house typologies owed a large debt to the deadpan techniques of artists like Graham, Ed Ruscha and, to a lesser extent, Andy Warhol. In addition, Scott Brown's association – through her education at the Architectural Association (AA) in London in the 1950s – with the Independent Group[5] also provided a common thread for an interest in popular culture.

Venturi and Scott Brown's 1976 exhibition 'Signs of Life' and their Yale studio Learning from Levittown were culminations of this interest in non-architect-designed residential buildings. The show was not a critical success,[6] and plans for a book – a follow-up to *Learning from Las Vegas*[7] – were shelved. In fact, Venturi and Scott Brown's interest in popular forms of American housing proved deeply problematic for architecture critics of all stripes.

'Signs of Life' used developments like Levittown (a New York housing development built between 1947 and 1951, widely considered to be the archetype for postwar suburbia) as source material for research into the changing forms of lower- and middle-class family housing. Venturi and Scott Brown suspended the kind of value judgements habitually made by architects when confronted with objects that did not conform to their own aesthetic prejudices, and tried to learn lessons that could be applied to their own designs. In doing so they drew heavily on the work of American sociologist Herbert Gans and, in particular, his book *Popular Culture and High Culture*, first published in 1974.[8] Gans had previously written about Levittown, and his studies of lower- and middle-class lifestyles led to an analysis of contemporary built culture based on taste.

According to Gans, there were a number of different taste cultures that broadly followed the layers of the class system. The stylistic and architectural preferences of the inhabitants of Levittown did not conform to the taste of architects and were thus denigrated as kitsch. Gans' sophisticated analysis of different taste cultures and the way they manifested themselves in architecture and interior design was a direct challenge to an architectural establishment that assumed the innate superiority of its own aesthetic preferences. More fundamentally it linked those aesthetic preferences to a specific socioeconomic class of which architects were usually a part. Gans' writing exposed the taste culture of architects as merely one of a number of competing and, sometimes, mutually antagonistic ones. It also suggested that if architects were to design successful housing, they would need to engage in taste cultures other than their own.

Gans' research is particularly useful when read in connection with Michel de Certeau's study of everyday life. If Gans is primarily interested in the production side of architecture – how architects tend to ignore the taste culture of the users of their buildings – then de Certeau is more concerned with how members of that culture might reinterpret the architecture they are offered.

Discussing the act of reading, de Certeau suggests that it 'has all the characteristics of a silent production: the drift across the page, the metamorphosis of the text effected by the wandering eyes of the reader, the improvisation ... of

venturi and scott brown
suspended the kind of value
judgements habitually
made by architects when
confronted with objects that
did not conform to their own
aesthetic prejudices, and tried
to learn lessons that could be
applied to their own designs.

taste is a sticky issue that brings with it issues of wealth, lifestyle and class.

meanings'.[9] De Certeau applies this idea to other everyday activities, contesting that the production of culture is never simply one-sided – that is, produced by someone and consumed by someone else – and that cultural objects are in a constant state of rereading and adaptation. Although he does not discuss do-it-yourself directly, it would seem to be an act of creative reinterpretation *par excellence*, and the home improver the embodiment of one of de Certeau's 'silent producers'.

According to Pierre Bourdieu, 'Taste classifies, and it classifies the classifier'.[10]

Taste is rarely, if ever, discussed in architecture, yet so much of how architecture is experienced from outside the discipline is bound up with it. Taste is a sticky issue that brings with it issues of wealth, lifestyle and class. In this sense, taste is a political issue. Viewed through the lens of taste, meaning in architecture is not universal but specific, the product of particular social, political and economic circumstances. Taste locates value on the surface of objects, that is on their cultural reception rather than on their innate properties.

Questions of taste become most acute in housing where the 'signs of life' that Venturi and Scott Brown observed are used to communicate personal value and meaning. What would happen if these things were seen as a creative part of the process rather than a degradation of architecture? If one took the rich panoply of applied DIY, of add-ons and adaptations and extensions as part of architecture's capacity for direct communicative meaning? Such a stance might conclude that architecture – at least in the case of housing – is not a static image of perfection, but a process enfolding over time.

A number of architectural shibboleths are involved in this shifting of value. Decoration, for instance, has only recently been rediscovered by architects, and its current use is carefully justified by the possibilities of computer-aided production techniques. More subtly, the temporal aspect of DIY raises profound questions over value. A history of DIY reveals the constantly shifting taste in domestic architecture, the modernising adaptations of one generation swiftly becoming insensitive additions for the next. Changes and adaptations of layout also describe shifts in family structure and social organisation. DIY is non-heroic and non-monumental. It implicitly acknowledges that tastes change and that nothing is sacred. Architecture's desire for permanence as much as its desire to transcend social conditions is challenged by the micro-histories and fashionable 'isms' of decoration.

The Architecture of Everyday Life

In 2003, FAT was commissioned to design 23 new homes for the residents of a soon-to-be-demolished council estate in Manchester. The Islington Square project (completed in 2006) embraced residents' taste and do-it-yourself as part of the design process, attempting to give expression to a taste culture normally marginalised by 'high' architecture and regeneration projects.

The process began with interviewing each resident in their existing home, taking photographs to record how these had been adapted over time. The alterations were both spatial and decorative, exuberant and subtle, ad hoc and carefully planned. Rooms had been reoriented and internal partitions demolished. A Hawaiian Beach Bar had appeared in the corner of a dining room. A non-functioning fireplace became the focal point for a living room. Additional layers of signage and decoration revealed micro-territories within the house or acted as expressions of ownership on the exterior.

Bastardised forms of decoration abounded; unpredictable conflations of adobe, mock Tudor, Rococo, Pop Baroque and hacienda style. A true horror show for architects, in other words. However, FAT approached this material not as a problem that needed clearing up, but as a source of inspiration. By avoiding moral/aesthetic value judgements, the office attempted to understand their functional, symbolic and decorative roles within the house. The subsequent design positions personal taste and owner adaptation as vital components of new housing. In doing so, the new houses became a question of taste as well as of space. The DIY taste of the residents became part of the design, giving vocal articulation to de Certeau's act of 'silent reading' and making it a form of public language.

FAT, Islington Square, New Islington, Manchester, 2006
below left: Islington Square completed.

below right: Resident's house 1. Resident adaptations of an existing house on the Cardroom Estate exhibiting a spectacular variety of styles (adobe, mock Tudor, hacienda), ornaments and decorative objects.

bottom left: Artist's impression produced for planning consultation showing the new Islington Square houses without resident modifications.

bottom right: Artist's impression produced for planning consultation showing the new houses with resident modifications.

opposite: Resident's house 2. The micro-territories within an existing house on the Cardroom Estate are made explicit by this piece of applied signage.

Beyond the mechanics of incorporating resident choice – the placing of internal partitions, choices of balcony position and so on – the design attempted to give spatial and typological expression to a social group often marginalised within urban regeneration projects. The residents, stated preference for suburban models of housing, combined with the required density of the development, suggested the development of a new, hybrid typology. The result combines the traditional 'northern' terrace with aspects of the semi-detached house and can be seen as either a terrace with a number of chunks taken out, or as a series of semi-detached units hidden behind a continuous facade.

The inclusion of items such as bird boxes and hanging baskets within the original design also subtly questions the limits of architecture. From a perceptual point of view, these additive elements suggest that the architecture is never finished, that its status is always in flux and open to change. The objects and decorative elements that float around the facade are like the ornaments within the residents' interiors, arranged temporarily and according to taste. They are neither the beginning nor the end of the process, and as such challenge the constraints and assumptions of both planners and architects.

The project explored tensions between taste cultures rather than privileging one over the other. The tastes of the residents and those of the client/developer enter into a creative conflict that recognises the partiality of both positions. The facade plays an important role in this, articulating the transition between the public realm of the city (and the requirements of the developer) and the private world of the interior (and the tastes of the residents). Instead of suppressing one behind the other, it becomes a space in which these various tensions are played out.

The scale of the facade relates to the future urban context, helping to mediate between the two-storey houses and the much taller apartment blocks planned for the rest of the development. The seemingly arbitrary shifts in colour of the oversized brick pattern relate to views of the houses as a whole

rather than to the units themselves. At the same time, the facade's parapet expresses each individual house as a separate entity. The decorative objects that accumulate on the surface of the facade further blur the distinction between public and private realms.

The design oscillates between traditional and contemporary, familiar and unfamiliar tropes. It develops a traditional typology – the northern terrace house – via the tastes of the predominantly working-class community of the area in a way that resists the gentrifying tendencies of redevelopment. Rather than ignoring the underlying social and economic tensions of regeneration, it foregrounds them, using taste as a method of asserting identity and meaning. ∆

Notes
1. Michel de Certeau, *The Practice of Everyday Life*, University of California Press (Berkeley, CA), 1984, pp xii–xiii.
2. Charles Jencks, *The Language of Post-Modern Architecture*, Academy Editions (London), 1977.
3. Michel de Certeau, op cit, p xii.
4. Dan Graham, *Rock My Religion: Writings and Projects 1965–90*, MIT Press (Cambridge, MA), 1993.
5. The Independent Group was an informal network of painters, writers and architects associated with the Institute of Contemporary Arts (ICA) in the early 1950s. The group – which included artist Richard Hamilton and architects Alison and Peter Smithson – was synonymous with an interest in the emerging consumer culture of the 1950s and regarded as a precursor to the US-based Pop Art movement.
6. For a thorough account of the critical reception to 'Signs Of Life', see Deborah Fausch, *Ugly and Ordinary: The Representation of the Everyday in Architecture of the Everyday*, eds Steven Harris and Deborah Burke, Princeton Architectural Press (New York), 2001.
7. Robert Venturi, Denise Scott Brown and Steven Izenour, *Learning from Las Vegas*, MIT Press (Cambridge, MA), 1972.
8. Herbert Gans, *Popular Culture and High Culture*, Basic Books (New York), 1999.
9. Michel de Certeau, op cit, p xxi.
10. Pierre Bourdieu, *Distinction: A Social Critique of the Judgement of Taste*, Routledge (London and New York), 1984, p xxix.

HISTORICISM VERSUS COMMUNICATION
THE BASIC DEBATE OF THE 1980 BIENNALE

The first Venice Architecture Biennale in 1980 provided a vital springboard for Post-Modernism, providing it with an international stage. The Strada Novissima, with its facades by eminent architects of the time, is now a seminal image of 20th-century architecture. As **Léa-Catherine Szacka** explains, the prominence given to the past in the show's theme was a point of contention among the exhibition's organisers. This has had an enduring impact on architectural culture to this day.

above: The multistranded exhibition included eight different sections. First were the entrance gate and the Teatro del Mondo, both temporary constructions by Aldo Rossi. After entering the Arsenale, visitors were treated to three homage exhibitions to Ignazio Gardella, Mario Ridolfi and Philip Johnson, as well as a historical display on the Corderie dell'Arsenale. Then came the famous Strada Novissima where a staircase

(behind Portoghesi's facade) led to the exhibition of the younger generation situated on the mezzanine floor. Also on the mezzanine was an exhibition dedicated to the Italian Neo-Liberty architect Ernesto Basile. At the end of the Strada Novissima was the Critics exhibition. Two small displays – Natura-Storia and L'Oggetto Banale – the latter curated by Alessandro Mendini and Studio Alchimia, were at the end of the route.

opposite: Visitors at the opening of the 'The Presence of the Past' exhibition in Venice on 27 July 1980. The exhibition was held in Venice's Corderie dell'Arsenale, an old and unused shipyard that was once the industrial heart of the city but never previously accessible to the public. The exhibition remained open until 19 October 1980.

In the summer of 1980, Venice became the theatre for the most important international architectural exhibition since the International Style was launched in Europe in 1927 at the Deutscher Werkbund exhibition in Stuttgart and then in New York in 1932 at the Museum of Modern Art (MoMA). For the Italians it was the audience more than the buildings that mattered. With roughly 40,000 paying visitors, the first Venice Architecture Biennale aimed at mass culture.[1] The event was based around the dual ideas of increasing communication and pluralism. Another significant emerging strand was historicism. It was, however, this emphasis on the past that became a point of contention between the people involved in organising the exhibition. What excited speculation was the current emergence of Post-Modernism[2] while the final title expressed the historicist ambition for 'The Presence of the Past'. It is a struggle that can be still observed some four decades later with many contemporary architects favouring communication and Prince Charles continuing to promote a traditional or historic approach.

When in 1975 Arthur Drexler staged 'The Architecture of the École des Beaux-Arts' show at MoMA, it was an enormous success. The strong Beaux-Arts tradition in the US meant that this historical exhibition struck a chord among the American public, awakening an interest in the classical while also opening up the possibilities of reinterpreting style. Five years later, the Italians, coming out of an economic boom that was pushing them towards consumerism, decided also to try to repeat the popularity of Drexler's architecture show by organising a large architecture exhibition, this time based around the highly contemporary Post-Modernism.

The Venice Biennale, an institution founded in 1895, is dedicated to various arts (dance, cinema, theatre, music, painting and sculpture) and provided a good platform for launching a lively architectural event aimed at a wider public. Curated by the charismatic Roman architect Paolo Portoghesi (also a noted historian of the Baroque), the exhibition was a multistranded display. Its main part, or at least that remembered most, was the Strada Novissima. In this artificial street, the plurality of propositions was so important that it revealed an unavoidable fact: there was no single 'ism' in Post-Modernism – it was a plurality rather than a unified style that Portoghesi and his team were putting forward to the world. The team was composed of Costantino Dardi, Rosario Giuffrè, Udo Kultermann, Giuseppe Mazzariol and Robert AM Stern, led by the critics Charles Jencks, Christian Norberg-Schulz, Vincent Scully and Kenneth Frampton.[3]

The exhibition was initially meant to emphasise communication, and the fact that, after years of Modern functionalism and abstraction, architecture had returned to narrative, to telling stories for its users.[4] Turning away from previous exhibits that presented nothing but the aesthetics of architectural photography, the curators of 'The Presence of the Past' wanted to put visitors in contact with architecture: to literally project them on to the street and into architecture.[5] It

was after looking at Charles Jencks' 1977 *The Language of Post-Modern Architecture*[6] that Portoghesi called the critic to take part in the exhibition's organisation. With his book, Jencks had made clear that Post-Modernism was about the return to language and communication. He put Minoru Takeyama's Ni-Ban-Khan building (Tokyo, 1970) on the cover in order to show the typical Pop mixed codes of Post-Modernism. From this paradigmatic example of a facade that communicates, to the end of the book with Antonio Gaudí, the most communicative of all architects, Jencks insisted on the need to return to language in architecture.

In Britain, the fate of Post-Modernism was ultimately determined by its association with historicism and the work of neo-classicists such as Léon Krier and Quinlan Terry under the patronage of Prince Charles. In the 1980s and early 1990s, high-profile projects such as Poundbury in Dorset, designed by Krier for the Duchy of Cornwall, and John Simpson's proposal for Paternoster Square, supported by the Prince, shifted interest away from communication and irony towards the recreation of 'authentic' traditional architecture and urban forms. This laid Post-Modernism wide open to the derision of the critics, as they disparaged it as little more than pastiche. It also meant that the original message about communication got smothered in the ensuing style wars as Post-Modernism was miscast as reactionary.

The title of the exhibition was modified many times. It varied between 'The Architecture of Post-Modern' to 'Dopo l'architettura moderna' ('After Modern Architecture') to 'Postmodern Architecture' to the very simple 'Postmodern' to 'La Mostra sul Postmodernismo' ('The Exhibition on Postmodernism') to an emphatic pronouncement, 'POSTMODERN'. Finally, inspired by the famous 1919 essay 'Tradition and the Individual Talent' by TS Eliot,[7] it adopted the title 'The Presence of the Past'. The reason for this was that the organisation committee deliberately chose not to use the word 'post-modern' at all, and subsequently bent the message of the exhibition towards historicism. Stern, the inclusivist, radically embraced many things, especially the past. Jencks went along with this shift in emphasis, while the unswerving Kenneth Frampton, committed to a revisionist Modernism, did not. He resigned at an early stage because of the formalism of certain architects and because he thought the exhibition was more anti-Modern than Post-Modern. Looking back in time, Portoghesi today claims, half nostalgic, half amused, yet with no bitterness: 'We had the illusion that it was something serious.'[8]

In order to determine who would be the main exhibitors on the Strada Novissima, this newest of streets, Portoghesi and his team held three meetings in Venice.[9] The list of architects, classified by their country of origin, included a lot of names. But, ultimately, and for many different aesthetic, ideological and political reasons, just 20 architects were short-listed.[10] Each member of the committee put forward his favourites. For instance, Norberg-Schulz chose Thomas Gordon Smith; Jencks advocated Frank Gehry and Rem Koolhaas; Scully convinced Robert Venturi to take part, and Portoghesi espoused Franco Purini and Ricardo Bofill, illustrating the many different tendencies flourishing at the time. Nine countries were represented on the Strada Novissima: six Europeans (Italy, the Netherlands, Spain, Germany, Luxembourg and Austria), the US and Japan. However, the bias of the countries represented is obvious when we examine where the organisers were from. Most countries had one or two (for Germany) representatives, while Italy had five and the US eight.

In this street of simulacra were many attitudes towards the past: but three basic tendencies stand out. The first, close to the ideology of Portoghesi, Stern, Scully or even Philip Johnson, was promoting the past *within* the present; a second, advocated by Aldo Rossi and Massimo Scolari, sought a timeless, atemporal architecture, a poetic architecture, where *neither past nor present* were emphasised; finally, a third faction, including Hans Hollein, Venturi/Scott Brown, Koolhaas and Jencks, highlighted irony and communication and promoted the past *and* the present. So if we leave aside the atemporal poetic 'dreamers' à la Rossi, the PoMo and others, we are left with a basic split. On the one hand were the historicists Greenberg, Gordon Smith (and partly) Bofill and Stanley Tigerman; on the other were those more committed to communication such as Koolhaas, Gehry, Michael Graves, Venturi/Scott Brown and Hollein. Some like Stern and Krier straddled these three attitudes, although both later on were to become clear historicists. So if Portoghesi had got the pluralism right,[11] he would have emphasised the differences between the major

attitudes (or many 'isms'), and proceeded to some sort of classification of facades. Since many attitudes were competing and the general public was little acquainted with Post-Modernism, the overwhelming diversity needed explaining: a pluralism made coherent.

Hollein's facade was, according to Jencks and other critics and architects, the most appropriate of all, because it used history and context ironically as double coding. It also avoided the rule that: 'the columns of the central nave cannot be part of the facade (they were to be 'covered')'. Thus it managed to be both critical of an easy historicism and in keeping with the immediate context. In addition to the two real columns, Hollein produced four artificial ones. One recalled the 1567 primitivist trunk of Philibert de L'Orme; another imitated Adolf Loos' famous project for the 1922 *Chicago Herald Tribune* column competition; one was covered by grass, and therefore a comment on the environmental crisis; and finally one pushed irony to its culmination by being hung in space, supporting nothing at all. This proved a crucial point of functionalism – it worked as the entrance. Surmounting the row of columns, Hollein employed a blue neon arch, a symbol of a gate or passageway. His facade was also a multiple linguistic entity, a play on several words besides 'the arch': for instance, the *Chicago Herald Tribune* was initially Loos' 'column' ('herald') with 'column-inches of text'. It was a simple yet effective Post-Modern communicative act. The architect did signal the return to the past, but put more emphasis on the communicative power of architecture, the way Jencks had defined Post-Modernism, as a language that had to communicate with various taste cultures.

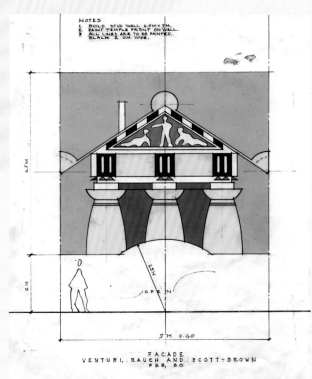

FACADE
VENTURI, RAUCH AND SCOTT-BROWN
FEB, 80

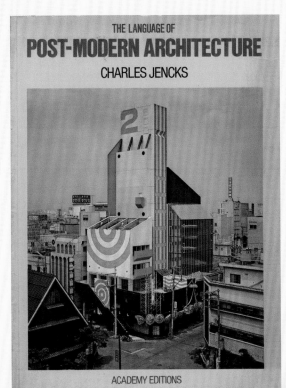

THE LANGUAGE OF
POST-MODERN ARCHITECTURE
CHARLES JENCKS

ACADEMY EDITIONS

The architect did signal the return to the past, but put more emphasis on the communicative power of architecture, the way Jencks had defined Post-Modernism, as a language that had to communicate with various taste cultures.

opposite: Drawing of Venturi, Rauch and Scott Brown's Strada Novissima facade sent to the Biennale in February 1980. The drawing gives basic indications for the construction of the facade.

top: Cover of the first edition of Charles Jencks' *The Language of Post-Modern Architecture* (1977). On the cover is Minoru Takeyama's Ni-Ban-Khan building in Tokyo, designed in 1970 and redesigned in 1977. The second edition of the book featured the redesigned building.

above: The Critics exhibition. In the middle of the room dedicated to the critical evaluation of Post-Modernism, Charles Jencks, with the help of Cinecittà technicians, built an immense 'leaning' pencil recalling the many leaning towers of the city of Venice. Each of the six facets of the pencil illustrated one trend of Post-Modernism. With the pencil came a sinking book on which was written 'all the wasms have become isms'. This white book was also used as a projection screen for Jencks' slide show on Post-Modern architecture.

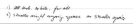

EUROPA(personali di architetti)

top: List of names with manuscript writing by Charles Jencks (found in his personal archive) and Robert Stern (found in the Venice Biennale archive). The lists were most probably distributed during the

second advisory commission meeting in November 1979. Certain names are crossed, others are circled. A few names have also been added.

above: The Strada Novissima. Left: Josef Paul Kleihues, Hans Hollein, Massimo Scolari and Allan Greenberg's facades. Right: Thomas Gordon Smith's facade seen through Greenberg's Serliana.

opposite: Hans Hollein's facade on the Strada Novissima.

Another successful facade was that by Krier, an architect who refused the film-set architecture of Cinecittà and insisted on building his flat edifice out of real materials. But even the best architect can be fooled. And Krier, in front of his facade made entirely in Cinecittà, shouted: 'Oh! But where did you find this real oak?'[12] The primitivist Krier was then a Post-Modernist defending the use of real oak against what some called 'pastiche'; that is, a kind of film architecture, a way of building fast and economically – just as Inigo Jones, Borromini and others had done before. The architecture of the Strada was not, as many deplored, mere pastiche. It was Cinecittà architecture, cinema architecture, a form of construction made for enhancing people's right to dream – still perfectly 'real'.

According to Portoghesi, Krier's was an example of what the facades were meant to be: more like houses, the houses of the personalities competing against each other. In that sense, the Strada Novissima was meant to be similar to Venice's Grand Canal, where the buildings share some elements while also being diverse, colourful and expressive. The Strada adhered to the rigidity of the grid, yet allowed individual liberties. And if one message transcended the actual Strada, it was pluralism. The aim, said the Italian Portoghesi, was to bring back the competition between architects, as in the 16th century and the Baroque period.

Mysteriously, some were absent from this large Post-Modern festival. Where were Peter Eisenman[13] and James Stirling?[14] Eisenman, later more of an abstract Deconstructivist, and his Institute of Architecture and Urban Studies (IAUS) in New York were against the idea, and vividly attacked the show. The French architect Christian de Portzamparc was to be part of the group, but his facade enigmatically disappeared from the Arsenale. It then reappeared in 1981, in the centre of Paris' Chapelle Saint-Louis de la Salpêtrière, to which the show next travelled. The Strada Novissima was there transformed into a circular piazza and Portzamparc was right in the centre, surrounded by a select group of others.[15]

In terms of international architectural politics, it was the reaction more than the action that created Post-Modernism, especially in Italy.[16] When the exhibition was presented in Paris, the reaction was even more vivid, giving rise to weekly debates in a boxing ring broadcast on television. After all, this exhibition was a polemical media event, and that is what made it famous and made it interesting. After this seminal 1980 exhibition, all subsequent architecture Biennales looked boring and did not raise any exciting mediated debate.

The 1980 exhibition, with its Strada Novissima, symbolised a sort of euphoric moment, the passage between two epochs, or as Gordon Smith would put it, a sort of 'Prague Spring'.[17] But in what way can it be regarded as prefiguring the radical prefix of this 2011 issue of △D? There are distinct aspects to it that have particular pertinence to a contemporary radical movement. First, it was radical as it proposed new techniques of display for architecture adapted to the emerging 'media world':

the model of the mall with 20 shopfronts for each architect's self-promotion. It expressed a radical pluralism in bringing together a wide cross-section of designers, yet asking them to share a common interest – a single street scene. There were thus different, even contradictory approaches within a single urban matrix. Through the exhibition, Portoghesi also admirably captured the spirit of the Arsenale, Venice's old naval shipyards. This was a radical act in so far as it opened to the public the Corderie, a vast three-aisled 16th-century workshop – one of the largest pre-industrial production spaces – that was dedicated to producing rope. It did so with an accessible and exciting show at an appropriately monumental scale. Through this public realm, the exhibition proposed a new type of space through a wholly Post-Modern treatment that still impacts on the way architecture is exhibited and consumed today.

In terms of its scale and success, the 1980 show was a radical departure: it was the first mediated large-scale international architecture exhibition with nearly 40,000 paying visitors in just three months. Moreover, it was far-reaching because of the contents of the show itself. Rather than being surrogates or representations of built work, the facades on the Strada Novissima were stand-alone pieces of architecture. Though they may not exist physically to this day, they continue to subsist in the memory of many visitors, and the image of the street in the Corderie has become a seminal one reproduced in architectural textbooks across the world.

If in the 1980s, in the immediate aftermath of the exhibition, communication became subsumed by historicism, in the long term the Biennale had the greatest impact through its realisation of architecture's ability to communicate. It is this potential to connect with a wider public that has sown the seed in the 21st century for a highly contemporary and 'radical' approach to Post-Modern architecture. Perhaps, as Gordon Smith predicted, these five swallows did make an Architectural Spring. △D

If in the 1980s, in the immediate aftermath of the exhibition, communication became subsumed by historicism, in the long term the Biennale had the greatest impact through its realisation of architecture's ability to communicate.

top: Léon Krier's sketch for his Strada Novissima facade.

above: The French version of the show, 'La présence de l'histoire: l'après modernité', was held at the Chapelle Saint-Louis de la Salpêtrière, Paris, from 15 October to 20 December 1981. Christian de Portzamparc's facade was an addition for the French show and was placed in the centre of one of the octagonal rooms of the chapel. Hans Hollein's facade can be seen in the background.

opposite: Léon Krier's facade on the Strada Novissima.

Notes

1. The Venice Biennale registered 36,325 paying visitors for 'The Presence of the Past' exhibition (a daily average of 526 visitors). Data from the historical archives of the Venice Biennale, Archivio Storico delle Arti Conteporanee (ASAC), historical file no 789/9. However, only paying visitors were counted, and it is likely that the real number was much higher. In an interview in March 2008, Paolo Portoghesi suggested that there might have been around 95,000 visitors. Another thing to consider is that, despite the Biennale these days attracting around 100,000 to 130,000 visitors, at the time even 40,000 was an unusually good attendance for an architectural exhibition.

2. Charles Jencks, interview with the author and Eva Branscome, 16 February 2009.

3. Frampton resigned from the organisation of the show in May 1980. A letter dated 13 May 1980 from Frampton to Robert AM Stern was found in the Robert AM Stern Architects Record, Manuscripts and Archives, at Yale University Library, Box 2, file 13. The letter explains in great detail the reasons for Frampton's resignation.

4. In an interview with the author and Eva Branscome on 16 February 2009, Jencks asserted that when he was first asked by Portoghesi to do the exhibition it was clearly going to be a show on the return of communication. Jencks says that it was only later that the message was shifted.

5. See Paolo Portoghesi's film *La Presenza del Passato*, directed by Maurizio Cascavilla, Radio Television Italia (RAI), 1980 (32 mins), in the historical archives of the Venice Biennale, Archivio Storico delle Arti Conteporanee (ASAC).

6. Charles Jencks, *The Language of Post-Modern Architecture*, Academy Editions (London), 1977.

7. 'Tradition is a matter of much wider significance. It cannot be inherited, and if you want it you must obtain it by great labor. It involves, in the first place, the historical sense, which we may call nearly indispensable to anyone who would continue to be a poet beyond his twenty-fifth year; and the historical sense involves a perception, not only of the pastness of the past, but of its presence; the historical sense compels a man to write not merely with his own generation in his bones, but with a feeling that the whole of the literature of Europe from Homer and within it the whole of the literature of his own country has a simultaneous existence and composes a simultaneous order. This historical sense, which is a sense of the timeless as well as of the temporal and of the timeless and of the temporal together, is what makes a writer traditional. And it is at the same time what makes a writer most acutely conscious of his place in time, of his contemporaneity.' TS Eliot, 'Tradition and the Individual Talent', 1919, first published in two parts in *The Egoist* in 1919, and later in Eliot's *The Sacred Wood* of 1920.

8. Paolo Portoghesi, interview with the author, 22 December 2010.

9. According to archival documents and to Robert AM Stern's diaries of 1979–80, the first one was on 14–15 September 1979, the second was on 23–24 November 1979, and the third on 1–2 February 1980.

10. The Strada Novissima exhibitors were (listed from the entrance to the end of the street): Costantino Dardi; Michael Graves; Frank O Gehry; Oswalt Mathias Ungers; Robert Venturi, John Rauch and Denise Scott Brown; Léon Krier; Josef Paul Kleihues; Hans Hollein; Massimo Scolari; Allan Greenberg (on the left side); Rem Koolhaas and Elia Zenghelis; Paolo Portoghesi; Ricardo Bofill/Taller de Arquitectura; Charles W Moore; Robert AM Stern; Franco Purini and Laura Thermes; Stanley Tigerman; Gruppo romano architetti urbanisti (GRAU); Thomas Gordon Smith; and Arata Isozaki (on the right side). The French architect Christian de Portzamparc was also part of the group, but for some mysterious reason his facade was not built in Venice.

11. He wanted pluralism from the beginning, as the text of the catalogue can prove.

12. Claudio d'Amato, interview with the author, 7 April 2010.

13. Eisenman today claims that although he was invited to exhibit, he rejected the offer on the advice of Manfredo Tafuri. Peter Eisenman, interview with the author, 16 June 2010.

14. Stirling had always been on the short list for the Strada. When asked about the absence of the English architect, Portoghesi recalls that Stirling never directly declined nor refused to take part, but simply said that he could not do it. According to Portoghesi, Stirling was by far the most notable absentee. Paolo Portoghesi, interview with the author, 22 December 2010.

15. According to Portoghesi and Francesco Cellini, Portzamparc, at the last minute, decided not to send a final drawing for the building of his façade, and only a preliminary version was printed in the exhibition catalogue. Paolo Portoghesi, interview with the author, 22 December 2010, and Francesco Cellini, interview with the author, 13 November 2010.

16. For the Roman architect and historian Bruno Zevi, the exhibition suggested a difficult leap towards building restoration. According to Zevi, Post-Modernism was nothing but a big pastiche that related to any historical style from Mesopotamian Egypt to Palladio; see 'Facciatisti e facciatosti, dibattito fra Paolo Portoghesi e Bruno Zevi', *L'Espresso*, 17 August 1980, pp 58–61. Vittorio Gregotti, the former director of the Biennale, also reacted in the press. He wrote in the *La Reppubblica* newspaper on 30 July 1980 that the Strada Novissima was nothing but an orgy of fake columns hiding the true, wonderful columns of the Arsenale. Further on he condemned the return of the *rue couloir* banished in the 1920s by Le Corbusier; see Vittorio Gregotti, 'I vecchietti delle colonne', *La Repubblica*, 30 July 1980. Finally, Jürgen Habermas said in 'Modernity: An Unfinished Project', the speech he gave when receiving the Adorno prize in Frankfurt in 1981: 'The response to this first architecture Biennale has been a disappointment.' See Jürgen Habermas, 'Modernity: An Unfinished Project', in Hal Foster, *The Anti-Aesthetic: Essays on Postmodern Culture*, 1st edn, Bay Press (Port Townsend), 1983, p 158. And although the philosopher only refers to the Biennale in his introduction, we now know that this event had been the departure point of a general reflection on the state of the Modern project as 'unfinished'. For Habermas, post-modernity equalled anti-modernity, and was opposed to the spirit of Adorno's work; he interpreted this cultural movement as the manifestation of a new conservatism.

17. Thomas Gordon Smith, interview with the author, 15 March 2010.

TOO GOOD TO BE TRUE THE SURVIVAL OF ENGLISH EVERYDAY POMO

'Intelligent, eclectic, witty, profoundly humanistic, and keen to debunk an inflexible, elitist and dangerously authoritarian Modernism': **Kester Rattenbury** evokes the spirit of early British Post-Modernism. She reminds us of how in the early 1980s it spearheaded a spirited community architecture that played a strategic role in protest against wholesale, motorway-led redevelopments and the survival of Convent Garden.

Farrell and Partners, Embankment Place,
London, 1990
opposite: 'It's behind you!': in the
late 1980s and early 1990s, Farrell's
Embankment Place took the role of
pantomime villain.

Covent Garden Housing Project (CGHP),
Newton Street Housing, Covent Garden,
London, 1980s
below left: Unsung, modest PoMo
has been the unremarked medium of
community architecture.

Martin Lazenby, Martlett Court, Covent
Garden, London, 1980s
below right: PoMo became the
recognisable 'brand' of community
architecture, as is apparent in this
scheme opposite the Royal Opera House.

It's ironic. For 30-odd years, PoMo has been the pantomime villain stalking the architectural scene: the scary monster you encouraged students to stay away from ('It's behind you!'). Meanwhile, the real ideals and tactics of Post-Modernism have sneaked around and taken over a big chunk of the polite, well-behaved, whispering architectural theatre.

Though not the approved view, this just seems like poetic justice: the revival (or survival) of one of the most ethical architectural movements of the last century. PoMo, in its pure early form, was intelligent, eclectic, witty, profoundly humanistic, and keen to debunk an inflexible, elitist and dangerously authoritarian Modernism.

But, just like idealist early Modernism, the developers gobbled it up, and everyone – including myself – went underground. 'I Am Not and Never Have Been a Post Modernist' said Robert Venturi, on the cover of *Architecture* magazine in May 2001;[1] wittily denying the later forms of a movement he well-nigh invented, while pointing up the witch hunt against PoMo (misquoting the anti-communist McCarthy era, in case you are under 30). In fact, Piers Gough says he is the only paid up PoMo-ist left. But something has gone wrong with the witch hunt. Everyone is doing decoration now. Everyone – from MVRDV to Peter Zumthor – is doing abstracted vernacular. We are far less absolute about 'authenticity'. Nobody is shy of historicism, references and quotes, not even the most fearsome Minimalists. Incredibly, even one or two parametricists – direct heirs of the most ruthless and self-obsessed bits of Modernism – say they love community involvement.

So in the UK, FAT has spent 20 years being alternatively fêted, attacked and dismissed as clever pranksters ('Are they *serious?*'). Branded by a long teaching association with them, I caught the edge of that abuse (marking panels and at *BD* Christmas parties). But now, the office's erstwhile opponents are adopting the very tactics they attacked. There is a distinct notion, in this issue's editorial meetings, of 'outing' these people, and making them eat their words.

In the Critical Shadow

It's tough to write in the shadow of Charles Jencks – that looming, chimeric, definitive PoMo figure, however charming and helpful he may be. In the discussions leading up to this publication, Jencks – in his curatorial role as co-guest-editor of this issue, strongly advocated his own take on an 'English' line of PoMo history, from which I partially diverge.

For Jencks, the spirit of 'English' PoMo is 'about' William Hogarth with his razor-sharp, shocking, pictorial exposition of society's ills. It begins with Alison and Peter Smithson's early adoption of Pop Art, their article 'But Today We Collect Ads,'[2] and their interest in the vernacular[3] – even though they went on to become the most Brutal and least Pop of their generation. It continues with 'Bowellism', a term coined by the enigmatic Mike Webb in his Furniture Manfacturers' Association Building (1957–8), a student project that drew him into the Archigram fold. Jencks went on to say that James Stirling, whose defection (roughly) from Brutalism to Post-Modernism in the 1970s and 1980s with projects like the Neue Staatsgalerie (1983) remains one of those pieces of architectural family history that get glossed over – even in the recent Stirling revival. In fact, he argues, the whole of English PoMo, taking in John Outram, Michael Wilford, Will Alsop, muf and FAT, is a suppressed area of history, which, like Hogarth, stuck in the craw of middle-class establishment good taste, and whose live exponents are unfairly excluded from the high architectural canon. This is true, but with provisos. First, Jencks' own *The Language of Post-Modern Architecture* (1977)[4] – the handbook of my generation – memorably criticised the Smithsons: Robin Hood Gardens (1972) was, let's face it, not nearly enough like the Georgian crescents of Bath; it was still grounded in a profoundly Modernist idea of city planning which didn't let people live in things that looked and worked like houses. With neat plurality, Jencks says he meant PoMo was about the 'Pop' Smithsons rather than the 'Brutal and Ordinary' ones. And he means it as a red rag to a bull. Smithsonians and Archigrammers typically hate PoMo and, conversely, they were exactly what my PoMo generation was reacting against.

Jencks is right: the Brutalism versus PoMo debate is a core paradox. The one takes base and everyday elements to the most austere high art; the other takes high culture (sometimes in corrupt form) into the everyday. It is a civil war whose internecine fury disguised its many, many shared concerns.

This dilemma is beloved of intellectuals and currently in the theoretical limelight.[5] But the whole argument feels unsuitably academic. English PoMo (as Jencks indeed suggests), evokes something flourishing centuries before Modernism. It is apparent not just in the late 16th-century Hardwick Hall, Humphry Repton's landscape designs and John Nash's architecture, but even more in innumerable ordinary houses:

perversity, borrowing, appliqué, a form of DIY and insouciant and cheeky or nostalgic adaptation apparent in both the 'lowest' and the 'highest' of architectural types. However, in its labelled form it is much more international, and it was entirely defined by Jencks, Venturi and Denise Scott Brown – two East Coast Americans and a South African. Early Dissenting chapels are absolutely decorated sheds. Dissent, emigration, ethical belief – and DIY – have been in it from the start.[6]

Most of all, trying to define Post-Modernism in terms of its 'High Code' currency, to win back its place in that hall of fame, feels like a bad fit. In the late 1970s and 1980s, Post-Modernism was, in its intentions and beliefs, essentially *anti*-high architecture. Defining its pure pedigree out of Brutalism and its twinship to High Tech is (academically) spot on, and completely beside the point. PoMo was, paradoxically, an attempt not to adopt the elite canon, and its survival (*pace* FAT and Gough) has been mainly outside the critical pale: developers' architecture and community architecture. And, it transpires, hidden in its favoured rivals.

The Disappearance of PoMo

From on the ground, it looked like this. When I started architecture school in the 1980s (OK, 1979), everyone was more or less Post-Modernist – whether or not you had capitals. PoMo embraced the queasy and the worthy: Philip Johnson's AT&T Corporate Headquarters in New York (1984) and Aldo van Eyck's then seminal Unmarried Mothers' Home in Amsterdam (1978). It included Venturi and Scott Brown's *Learning from Las Vegas* (1972),[7] but also Bernard Rudofsky's *Architecture Without Architects* (1964).[8] It was quite friendly to classicism and closely related to High Tech, which, with its playfulness, expressiveness and lateral thought had developed in parallel. (Remember the Farrell Grimshaw Partnership before the partners went their own ways? Or that useless cross-bracing on Team 4's Reliance Controls?) It was decidedly for the user. It allowed access to architectural design for anyone who cared to get involved.

My own comic opera, staging the rise and fall and rise of UK PoMo, is set around Covent Garden and begins in 1974 – not necessarily the definitive scenario, but the one I watched being played out and can revisit in the most detail, and certainly the one which took a lot of the limelight. The old fruit-and-vegetable market had moved to Nine Elms, and the area was to be cleared. Unbelievably, now that Covent Garden is an icon of urban-regeneration schemes the world over, more than two-thirds of the whole area was to be demolished by the Greater London Council (GLC), including the market building itself.

The GLC was planning a network of inner-city ring roads right across London: flyovers, deck access and walkways. Hammersmith, the Westway, the A102M would be everywhere. However much we love it now, Robin Hood Gardens was then an intrinsic part of a really scary environmental problem. PoMo was part of the language of architectural protest against terrifying wholesale, motorway-led redevelopments – state and private.

The Covent Garden Community Association's protest, organised by hundreds of local businesses and residents, fought its way through an unsympathetic planning process to overturn the plan; to get the market restored and working, to get a hundred-odd buildings listed, and for an area plan which protected local residents, businesses and buildings. Like New York's Greenwich Village campaign (with Jane Jacobs in the 1960s), it changed the landscape for planning and cities worldwide.

The local community architectural practice, the Covent Garden Housing Project (CGHP), which grew out of this, was one of many which used a low-key PoMo precisely as a contextual user-negotiation with the 'high culture' of architects. By the time the Prince of Wales noticed community architecture in the 1980s, soft PoMo was its well-established style. Its most famous UK example – using the definition 'PoMo' inclusively, as it appeared then – was Ralph Erskine's Byker Wall (1969–74).[9] It has gone on being used for making user-friendly social housing ever since – unsung, everyday, some good, some bad – way out of fashion and rarely published. Indeed, community architecture was later cold-shouldered because it was PoMo.

It was often modest. An important, almost invisible early example was at Comyn Ching Triangle at Seven Dials (1978–85), just north of the Covent Garden market. This was a clever, lateral conversion and reuse of existing buildings into a mixed-use live-work-shop development, with some PoMo twists. It was by Terry Farrell, then the darling of both community architecture, PoMo-ists and a kind of lateral, Archigrammy High Tech. Only later would that seem an impossible combination.

But by the early 1980s, the 'High' debate of Post-Modernism was building up. Farrell's still-Archigrammy, Clifton Nurseries 1 (1980), a self-build, pop-up, eco-friendly curvy greenhouse, had been put up by students and volunteers in Bayswater, to rave reviews. But with Clifton Nurseries 2, back at Covent Garden (1981), the heat was rising. Clifton Nurseries 2 was another temporary building, on the site of what was to become the Royal Opera House extension (already the area's hot potato). That site offered a particular contextual challenge: one of London's strongest and most mixed classical settings, it faced the great facade of St Paul's Church across the square. And yet it was a cheeky temporary garden centre project – Liza Doolittle at the Opera.

Farrell's scheme was really brilliant: another cheap polycarbonate shed (still an unfamiliar material), it had twice the front it should have done. It formed a big-yet-small portico, which was half entrance and half billboard, the billboard half more solid and classical than its 'real' mirror, with swags of real foliage and trees standing in for their stone surrogates. Lateral, cheeky and punching about its weight (as market buildings ought to), it still seemed shocking in its stage-classicism – an overtly ambiguous adoption of an establishment language.

Farrell had been the darling of English PoMo in its radical-rethink role – he designed the 'alternative' proposal to Peter Palumbo's Mies van der Rohe scheme at Mansion House (1988) – but things would not stay that way. Farrell never saw

**Farrell and Partners, Comyn Ching
Triangle, London, 1985**
Farrell's modest, intelligent and witty reuse
of an urban block scheduled for demolition.

developers as the enemy, though he was playing in a world where 'commercial' was a dirty word. PoMo was seen – roughly – as the community's weapon against large-scale commercial development. (There was AT&T, of course, but that was a long way away, and we hoped it wasn't true.)

When the vast forms of Embankment Place, a big commercial PoMo development completed in 1990, began rising on the skyline just south of Covent Garden, Farrell's community and lateral fans (like me) went into shock. (Ironically, the opposite shock Modernists felt about Johnson's AT&T.) Farrell seemed to have sold PoMo – the secret weapon of the architectural left – down the river.

The sense of outrage that was expressed at this sturdy piece of urban massing seems more indecipherable now. But our reaction brings us back to Hogarth. To a certain extent, 'real' PoMo does seem to be about protest, about satire, about the accommodation of opposites. The many developers who gobbled PoMo up presumably noticed its relative economy and its power as a 'rebrand' – suggesting the building was community friendly, whatever the reality. So something in our reaction was right. There is a peculiar death of 'real' PoMo when it becomes part of the establishment.

The other big example was just east of Covent Garden in Trafalgar Square. In 1984, the Prince of Wales had weighed in with a (roughly) Post-Modernist argument: 'Why can't we have those curves and arches which express feeling in design? What is wrong with them?'[10] In the rumpus and massive disruption of plans around Trafalgar Square that his intervention caused, bizarrely, we ended up with a proposal for the National Gallery extension by our old PoMo heroes: Venturi, Scott Brown and Associates (VSBA). In retrospect, it was a brilliant decision for posterity, but boy didn't the architectural community hate VSBA then. It seemed all wrong for the time. After years in the doghouse, British High Tech had emerged with truly spectacular and (arguably) contextual pieces of world-class

innovation. Richard Rogers Partnership's Lloyd's of London and Foster + Partners' Hong Kong and Shanghai Bank, opened in 1986. High Tech now looked like our best hope to reinvent commercial development and public buildings – and now its unreliable twin was ranged against it.

Worse still, the Sainsbury Wing (1991) was a prime example of that painful new Thatcherite policy – the replacement of state funding for the arts with corporate sponsorship.[11] So the National Gallery extension, with its functional and witty assessment of the urban situation, and with all VSBA's ethical and community credentials, ended up 'representing' not just the monarchy, but Thatcherism too. We were all burning our metaphorical PoMo cards as fast as we could.

Even more interesting was what was happening at Covent Garden itself. A victim of its own success, commercial pressure was stretching the local plan to the limits, and by the early 1980s the Opera House's super-canny board of cultured developers and critics were ahead of the changing world. They were going for a part commercially funded extension, turning their backs on the principle of sole state funding for the arts, seeking the demolition of several listed buildings including the Grade 2 listed Floral Hall, and a relaxation of the area plan. They were upping the commercial content big time, changing planning law for commercial gain. And, aware of the power of architectural correspondents in a newly architecturally aware Britain, they had picked Dixon Jones – a practice they quite rightly thought everyone would like.

Dixon Jones were certainly pluralists. Jeremy Dixon had done tin box, High Tech-y housing at Milton Keynes, and Dixon Jones had done out-and-out PoMo at Westbourne Park. In the new world they were becoming Neo-Modernist-ish – and they had done it all beautifully without annoying anyone. The 16-year embattled redesign of the Royal Opera House was, it now seems, one of the places where PoMo survived by going into deep cover.

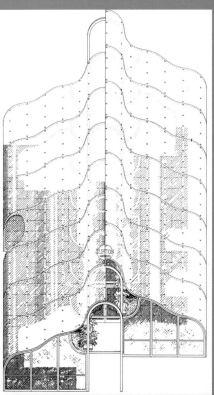

THERE IS A PECULIAR DEATH OF REAL POMO WHEN IT BECOMES PART OF THE ESTABLISHMENT

Carl Laubin, *Royal Opera House Covent Garden*, London, 1986
below: Looking from the loggia across Covent Garden Piazza, this image includes a number of key characters from the period as portraits: Charles Jencks, James Stirling, James Gowan, Terry Farrell, Leon Krier, Andrea Papadakis (the publisher of Δ at the time) and Fenella Dixon.

Dixon Jones, Royal Opera House, Covent Garden, London, 1999
bottom: A great assembly of types and tactics, and the place where Post-Modernism went underground.

Dixon Jones, St Mark's Housing, North Kensington, London, 1979
opposite: From the days when PoMo was clearly an ethical, contextual, humane and witty form of more-than-acceptable Modernism.

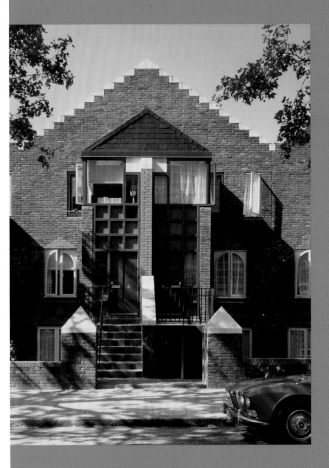

Art Gallery, Walsall (2000) – years before Caruso St John came out all lacy in the Nottingham Contemporary Arts Centre (2009). It is apparent in all kinds of aspects of the everyday – community credentials and all.

This issue of Δ was originally subtitled 'The Return of Communication'. 'Where from?' you might wonder. Because Minimalism, like Modernism (as Venturi and Scott Brown pointed out) was nothing if not communicative. And anyhow, communication was only one of PoMo's weapons: cunning, subterfuge and sheer ethics were at least as important. The vanishing and quiet re-emergence of PoMo was a brilliant tactic to escape its inappropriate establishment trap. It doesn't matter what people call it, the everyday is fine so long as we use its lateral, economical tactics to reinvent, to challenge its new big targets – which remain, basically, a ferocious commercial imperative; but now most evident in a criminally lazy overuse of energy, and a terrifying parametric urbanism (a new generation of would-be heroic, we-can-do-it form-making now flooding the up-and-coming student agenda), which threaten to repeat all the mistakes of modern planning at an even more scary scale. It is not just the pluralist medium that should be welcomed back, but the message. Δ

Notes
1. See, with cover, Robert Venturi, 'A Bas Postmodernism, Of Course', *Architecture*, Volume 90, Number 5, May 2001, pp 154–7.
2. Alison and Peter Smithson, 'But Today We Collect Ads', *Ark*, No 18, November 1956.
3. And, I would add, their amazingly eclectic books – from the Euston Arch protest to their children's books, *The Tram Rats*.
4. Charles Jencks, *The Language of Post-Modern Architecture*, Academy Editions (London), 1977.
5. For instance, the excellent new anthology, *Neo-Avante-Garde and Postmodern*, edited by Mark Crinson and Claire Zimmerman, Yale University Press (New Haven, CT), 2010, which deals precisely and deliberately with high-code academic concerns.
6. And to conclude the Jencks argument, while I agree that those dubbed as PoMo have often been abused, I find it hard to buy that Farrell, Gough or Coates have been suppressed or excluded from publicity.
7. Robert Venturi, Denise Scott Brown and Steven Izenour, *Learning from Las Vegas*, MIT Press (Cambridge, MA), 1972.
8. Bernard Rudofsky, *Architecture Without Architects*, MoMA/Doubleday (New York), 1964.
9. The scheme replaced prewar back-to-back housing in the Byker district of Newcastle with a mainly low-rise and humane approach, including the on-site architects' office distributing garden seeds and so on.
10. The Prince of Wales said this during his famous 'carbuncle speech' when he referred to Richard Rogers' scheme for the National Gallery as 'a monstrous carbuncle on the face of a much-loved and elegant friend'. It was given at the 150th anniversary of the Royal Institute of British Architects (RIBA), Royal Gala Evening at Hampton Court Palace, on 29 May 1984. For full transcript see: www.princeofwales.gov.uk/speechesandarticles/a_speech_by_hrh_the_prince_of_wales_at_the_150th_anniversary_1876801621.html.
11. As its name suggests, the construction was financed by a bequest from the founding family of the supermarket chain.

The Opera House is an amazing, eclectic assembly of types: the old restored theatre; a stunning, vast secret backstaqe; and a magically expanding foyer, shouldering the relocated Floral Hall. It is a piece of urban scenery. It was the first use of those astonishing hybrid images by Carl Laubin: an 18th-century-style painting over computer-generated images, giving a synthetic, teched-up traditionalism that the completed buildings eerily mimic. At one point, the Opera House had a 'Modernist' corner – arguably the only use of Modernism as overt PoMo appliqué in an architectural world then immersing itself in 'honest' Neo-Modernism. It was, however, scrapped in the many redesigns. The visibly thin stone cladding punctured with round windows, which is there now, was PoMo's final wave goodbye. The Royal Opera House was where PoMo went underground.

And very, very successfully. It can be argued that PoMo's strong, catholic re-emergence from the 'whisperers' now is because many of those original ideals were carried for years by just those people deemed to hate PoMo. You can find it in Tony Fretton's refined facades of the Lisson Gallery (1992), which was produced by drawing and redrawing the facades of neighbouring newsagents. You can find it in Caruso St John's Arte Povera expression of a ruined terraced house in the New

THE TRUE COUNTERFEITS OF BANKSY
RADICAL VVALLS OF COMPLICITY AND SUBVERSION

Tattoo or consummate object of consumption? Banksy's artwork has an uneasy status. It simultaneously has the power to subvert, questioning the conventions of the art world while potentially colluding with it. **Eva Branscome** explores the paradox of Banksy in the light of Post-Modernism.

In the summer of 2009, an average of 4,000 people a day came to see the provocative exhibition 'Banksy versus Bristol Museum' at the City Museum and Art Gallery, Bristol. Banksy exemplifies the Radical Post-Modernism of this issue, as illustrated explicitly by the 'versus' in the title of his show. He turns today's cities and streets into galleries and, by contrast, transforms museums into shrines of pop culture and commentary on the art market. Thus he subverts the usual status of both urban street and gallery. Today graffiti and street art occupy a space between cultural criticism, art and vandalism, which can, if used effectively, provide an opportunity for significant meaning. Yet it is also difficult to locate Banksy exactly. When the jester rules the court, it is hard to tell when subversion of the system becomes cynical complicity. This blur or confusion has a lesson for a Post-Modernism trying to become more radical.

Banksy's early work in the 1980s was more clearly graffiti, even vandalism. But the freehand, multicoloured sprayed pieces of urban hieroglyphics were extended by the mid-1990s with the new use of the stencil. The stencil allows super-quick visual messages to be applied to the walls. The images are usually no more than two-tone – black spray working with a lighter background. Sometimes an accent of colour is added. Most of the preparation happens beforehand and so avoids the danger of detection that is the risk of a slower freehand piece. While Banksy was not the first to adopt the stencil for street art, and his early work is clearly inspired by the American conceptual artist Jenny Holzer, the Bristol boy has used this minimalist style of wall decoration way beyond his sources. He has opened up the genre of 'high-street irony', playing with words and images. The pieces are disarmingly funny and that is key to Banksy's success.

In a piece that went up in Islington in 2008 he mixed kitsch nostalgia with issues of racism and commerce. Three sweet little patriotic children are taking part in a flag-raising ceremony. It could be a Norman Rockwell painting, except that it is a stencil and one of the kids is black and the banner is a Tesco bag. Another mural, shown in London at the Cans Festival of urban art organised by Banksy in May 2008, depicts an employee from the London graffiti-cleaning crew in his typical day-glo orange jacket pressure-spraying what looks like a prehistoric cave painting.

But Banksy's street art has developed still more complexity. While it no longer patiently builds up coloured layers, it works as a carefully orchestrated apparatus that targets a market of otherwise untapped art lovers to subvert everyday expectations. It stokes the collectors' interest through the mischief of public spectacles, the subversion of clichés and convention.

Street Art as a Radical Book

Banksy has made money through the sale of his book *Wall and Piece,* originally published in 2005.[1] It was the bestseller within its category for individual artists, completely surprising a stagnant art book market, selling 90,000 copies and taking £1 million – one-seventh of an entire market worth £7 million.[2]

Filled with acts of 'vandalism', the book is, importantly, aesthetically driven. Words and street image are conceived together to unfold as a narrative. There are five basic stories, each of which dramatises a sequence of carefully staged and photographed street graffiti. The captions are not incidental; every page sends a double message. In effect, Banksy transforms the lesson learned from the book narrative to the street wall and back to the pages of the book.

The book's layout is ingenious, the photographs perfect in terms of lighting, composition and complete with bin bags and debris that add grit and credibility to the scenes. If you look carefully, however, even the 'coincidental' pedestrians in the photos can be interpreted as commenting on the Banksy piece to which they are juxtaposed. Possibly these images are just a bit too perfect. Who has taken them anyway? Could they be posed?

The main five themes critiqued in the *Wall and Piece* include modern behaviour, the treatment of animals and stunts at international museums – interventions at the Tate in London and the Museum of Modern Art (MoMA) in New York that subvert normal canons of value. Politically Banksy has taken on the situation in Palestine, the police state in Britain, and rats and monkeys everywhere.

He likes the monkeys for their human characteristics; they are a metaphor. We are all monkeys is what Banksy is actually saying, and we could be fools. A picture story that appears at the very beginning of the thick book shows the escape of an ape from the laboratory of intelligence testing. It is a radical challenge for people to subvert the system by using its own tools against it. It is an introduction and justification for

Banksy, *Street Cleaner*, Cans Festival,
Leake Street, London, 2008
below: An act of vandalism: the London
graffiti-removal man is cleaning away
cave paintings.

Banksy, *I pledge allegiance to the bag*,
Islington, 2008
bottom: The children here are dedicated to
consumerism. The flagpole is part of the
impromptu wiring installation of the actual
building and illustrates the site-specific in
Banksy's work.

... depicts an employee from the london graffiti-cleaning crew in his typical day-glo orange jacket pressure-spraying what looks like a prehistoric cave painting.

117

Banksy, 'Simple intelligence testing', from *Wall and Piece*, 2005
bottom: On the flip side of this double-page spread picture sequence, the monkey eats the banana, stacks the boxes on top of each other and escapes through a ventilation shaft in the building.

Banksy, *Double yellow lines*, Tower Hamlets, London, 2007
below: The road worker's out-of-control double yellow lines present the people of Tower Hamlets with a gigantic flower.

the application of Banksy's own politically interventionist art practices that follow.

Banksy's book appeals to the middle-class urbanites and is for sale not just in bookstores. You can find it in trendy shops selling clothing and skateboard equipment, but also in urban lifestyle boutiques. It has become its own sort of trademark for edginess and urban chic. The book market is flummoxed by the phenomenal sales it has brought in: 'the ongoing success of Banksy's *Wall and Piece* proves that there is mass-market appeal for at least a particular type of art book. And the public demonstrably have an interest in art. It should perhaps not escape retailers' notice that people are continuing to go to museums and galleries in record numbers.'[3] A strange statement indeed as Banksy's work is for sale only at select galleries and had not really been officially on show at museums at the time this was published. He is not a mainstream modern artist and is still very much counterculture.

So who is Banksy? The persona or brand is carefully positioned. It portrays a young hoodie, moving quickly in a world of shadows, dodging CCTV cameras while the adrenaline rush guides his spray can, a glamorised subversive superhero. But perhaps Banksy is the art world's Wizard of Oz – an unimposing middle-aged man working a clever apparatus. The evident art world references and the sophistication of narratives imply that he is not under-educated. Is he possibly a copy editor or a Royal Academician? His work appears neither naive nor self-taught, and his anonymity as controlled as that of Greta Garbo.

Banksy understands his market, and runs a lucrative enterprise; his street pieces immediately feature in London's *Evening Standard*. Some are real, some are fakes. This opposition is essential to the mystique. But the most adept of Banksy's fan club have already been on location, taken their pictures and posted them in various cyber-forums as evidence. A mixture of good eyes and tip-offs from Banksy's machine guided them there. They take delight in being insiders and quicker than the press.[4]

Social Contradictions: The Sanctioned Outlaw

Just another example of this sort of manipulation is the fact that Banksy's walls are now often legally sanctioned, agreed beforehand in clandestine negotiations with the owners. A 'Banksy' gives added value to a wall, especially in London's Tower Hamlets. The paintings are done behind draped scaffolding. When overnight the scaffold comes down, the 'Banksy' magically appears. Then prints based on these images are made and sold. The obsession for these reproductions and the recording of the ultimately ephemeral appearance of renegade art through photography are reminiscent of the collection of relics from a pilgrimage – the oldest form of tourism. Just as you can take some water from Lourdes or bring back the leaning tower of Pisa in a snow globe, our fans want a piece of Banksy and they can buy it or save it on a memory chip.

If we consider just the monetary aspects, such street-wise behaviour makes Banksy's work appear cynical. But there is usually a clear social message that critiques mainstream assumptions, either of the art market or politics. In 2007 at the Christmas event he organised in Bethlehem, Banksy declared the Palestinian side of the Separation Wall a street art site. In 2008 he went to New Orleans with his stencils to draw attention to an embarrassingly large and mysteriously under-represented section of the displaced poor still living in temporary accommodation – three years after Hurricane Katrina's devastation. He has forced an engagement with the modern art establishment by hanging up fakes in international museums that were only discovered hours later, and sparring with Damien Hirst conceptually by using living animals as his canvas/wall performance art. In 2007 he defaced Hirst's *Pharmaceutical* spot painting with a stencil chambermaid seemingly lifting part of the canvas, emptying her dustpan behind it and exposing the framework. This new piece was called *Keep it Spotless*, and fetched $1,870,000 at Sotheby's auction in New York in 2008. This was a collaboration though, and not an actual act of vandalism. Hirst had organised the auction as a charity event and asked Banksy to contribute. Banksy's response had been for Hirst to send over one of his works so he could do something with it. Again, clever manipulation.

So, has Banksy joined the ranks of collusion where the artist and art market are incestuously intertwined? Is he, like Damien Hirst, allowed to get away with buying his own work to boost its value? In no other economic sector is this kind of thing allowed. Antitrust laws and those against insider trading are meant to prevent it. But, there is no doubt that the days of innocence in art are long gone, if they ever existed.

so who is banksy? the persona or brand is carefully positioned. it portrays a young hoodie, moving quickly in a world of shadows, dodging cctv cameras while the adrenaline rush guides his spray can, a glamorised subversive superhero.

Banksy, *Armoured Peace Dove*, Palestine, 2007
below: The dove in Palestine is wearing a bulletproof vest; still, the crosshairs of a visor are aiming at its heart. Does peace stand a chance in these war-torn lands?

Banksy, *Homage to Keith Haring*, Southwark, London, 2010
centre: The anonymous street artist shows his respect for what is arguably the most recognised graffiti image.

Banksy, *One Nation under CCTV*, Newman Street, London, 2008
bottom: A security guard photographing a hoodie kid with a paint roller. Note the real CCTV on the wall.

graffiti is still about marking territory and rejecting the power implications of the built environment.

In the 1960s the critic Arthur Danto proclaimed that after Warhol's Brillo box, anything could be a work of art. Banksy's urban interventions, like no other contemporary art, put pressure on the official system of collection, gallery and museum. He plays with the concept of art, mixing it up with vandalism and adding a significant dash of sophisticated marketplace. But has Banksy overstepped his boundaries, has his subversion become complicity?

A Thing of Hybrid Taste Cultures

Banksy's work, his exhibitions and prints and 'legal' street vandalism are in many ways attacking the cult of Warhol and simultaneously raising two fingers to Brit Art as well. But no one is yet treating this seriously. If graffiti is a Post-Modern language of street communication sending messages from the disenfranchised to the powerful, then Banksy is its most radical artist. Graffiti acts as a critique of the alienated spaces of modernity, and thus shows up in car parks, derelict industrial sites and the underbellies of highway overpasses – the residual areas of a dehumanised infrastructure. The abused street and the derelict urban district are its natural habitat, and concrete is its canvas. As a form of Radical Post-Modernism, graffiti is about heightening communication and occurs on several levels. It means one thing to the passer-by, something different to locals, and something else to those who read about it or see it collected in a gallery.

Like Post-Modernism generally, this renegade art form flowered in the 1980s and was second cousin to gang culture, clubs and drugs. But graffiti grew from these beginnings and developed naturally from streetwise to market-savvy. As an art form now its subject matter is more self-referential than territorial, more self-portraiture than 'Kilroy was here'. Although it is still about marking location, street art now increasingly likes to feature itself and its paraphernalia, the spray can and its archenemy, the ever-present CCTV camera. And it is aware of its own history paying homage to its predecessors such as Keith Haring.

This has been a gradual development since about 1990 where the interest slowly becomes surface and context. The positioning of street art is often carefully chosen and the designs frequently site-specific – like mainstream Post-Modernism. Graffiti works with the colour schemes of the surroundings, or plays with existing architectural shapes. It can extend to performance when artists arrange to work together, painting, then

if graffiti is a post-modern language of street communication sending messages from the disenfranchised to the powerful, then banksy is its most radical artist.

photographing or filming the process, making a permanent record of ephemerality. This worldwide phenomenon has led to graffiti tourism, where a travelling artist will leave his 'Kilroys' behind. While his works are shown in urban galleries he will more than likely also leave his mark on the streets, thus upping his recognition and market value.

But discussing street art along with mainstream art, architecture and urban planning will inevitably lead to the departure of the professionals and the middle class. It remains very much beyond the pale, like a tattoo, a sign of being unspeakable. Infringing on the body of the city it contains an implicit critique of location. Graffiti is still about marking territory and rejecting the power implications of the built environment. Because of this we have no serious interpretation of this radicalising art form. It is like the argument between calling someone a freedom fighter or a terrorist; there is symmetry but no common ground or willingness to talk. Graffiti manifests the emergence of another taste culture, one well below the five that the urban sociologist Herbert Gans distinguishes.[5]

Banksy is the movement's mover; like the typical Post-Modernist he uses the establishment against itself. He turns the art market on its head by using the city as his gallery, and renders the police and planning officers ineffective by negotiating legal walls. His teachers are Agitprop and Dadaism, Le Corbusier, Hogarth and Beardsley. This is 'subversion from within' and, by doing this, Banksy's work manages to hold up a double mirror to society. But Banksy is a hybrid thing: both in his acts of subversion and his complicity with the system, his work ultimately questions our taste cultures. While his canvas is the surface of the city, its walls, this necessarily also poses the question: Is there no Banksy in architecture? ⌂

Notes
1. Banksy, *Wall and Piece*, Century (London), 2005, pp 16–19.
2. Tom Nivan, 'Art of the Matter', *The Bookseller*, 8 June 2009. See: www.thebookseller.com/in-depth/feature/87829-art-of-the-matter.html.
3. Ibid.
4. This information is based on many conversations with art collector and photographer Eddiedangerous between 2007 and 2011.
5. Herbert Gans differentiates between 'high culture', 'upper-middle culture', 'lower-middle culture', 'low culture' and 'quasi-folk low culture' in his chapter 'The Five Taste Publics and Cultures' in *Popular Culture & High Culture: An Analysis and Evaluation of Taste*, rev edn, Basic Books (New York), 1999, pp 100–19.

re-radicalising post-modernism

Sean Griffiths, Charles Holland and Sam Jacob of FAT look back in retrospect at their top-ten Post-Modern moments. In a selection, which spans Denise Scott Brown looking vibrant in Las Vegas to James Stirling's exquisite drawing of the Derby Civic Centre and OMA's ingenious strip for the Parc de la Villette, they remind us of the dynamic radicalism of some of the period's greatest protagonists.

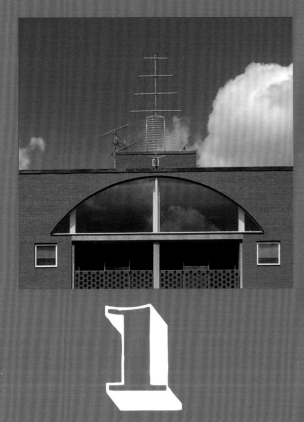

Venturi, Scott Brown and Associates, Guild House Antenna, Philadelphia, Pennsylvania, 1964

On the top of the old people's home, taking the place traditionally occupied by a religious statue, the golden, overscaled TV aerial makes a statement about electronic communication and physical space. The super-sizing and material coding of this piece of broadcast infrastructure is both functional and symbolic. Just as Chuck Berry had sung about radio in a secular musical form derived from religious origins, the Guild House aerial can be read as an acknowledgement of the complex relationship between architecture and the buzz of communicational networks. More specifically, it asks us about the relationship of architecture to media.

1

2

Denise Scott Brown in the desert off the Las Vegas Strip, 1967

There is no more powerful image of the architect than Denise Scott Brown standing next to the rubble of a collapsed hut in the desert with fragments of the Las Vegas Strip on the horizon. In it can be seen the foundation of an entirely different image of the architect as real, true humanist. It is an image of energy, engagement and a willingness to take on the reality of urban conditions, however complex, confusing and challenging.

Arata Isozaki & Associates, Tsukuba Centre Building, watercolour depicting the centre in ruins, 1979–83

3

While we lament architecture's lost cultural significance, Isozaki's full-on narrative overload takes on the history of the world. From Michelangelo to apocalypse, Isozaki reconfigures architecture as a communicative media outstripping all but the most extreme manga with its claustrophobic intensity. Architecture's insistence on abstraction is its own choice. Isozaki shows how embedding explicit narrative in the fabric and language of architecture can perform as a critique – even of itself. A way of architecture articulating its opposition to the very forces that bring it into the world.

James Stirling, Derby Civic Centre, 1974

4

History and conservation, but with an edge so sharp that it ensures that everyone would be offended. By retaining a historic facade, yet laying it at an impossible angle, Stirling reconfigures the site's context. He reveals that we can understand architecture's role, and not only as an act of construction. Closer to Gordon Matta-Clark's architectural interventions, the existing built environment becomes the site of an operation that reveals both the subtexts of our culture and the potential for its transformation.

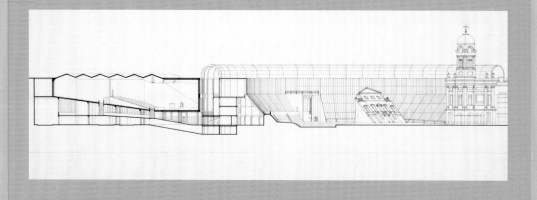

Charles Moore, Santa Barbara Faculty Club interior, 1968

Charles Moore's work challenges the criticism of Post-Modernism as anti-spatial. His projects explore fragmented, layered spatialities, taking the collage sensibility of early Modernism – Picasso's Cubism, Kurt Schwitter's Merzbau – and combining it with an interest in popular culture and everyday architecture. His work is a three-dimensional form of Pop Art that reaches its apogee in the interior of the Santa Barbara Faculty Club. Here, a strange, twisted geometry creates a compaction of routes, stairs and walkways looping back on themselves like a Beaux-Arts plan designed by MC Escher. Views through cartoonish cut-out walls, mock baronial trumpets with neon signs like unfurled banners, Rococo tapestries and Modernist marine detailing compete within an object that is in the Spanish hacienda style by way of Alvar Aalto. This is the high point of PoMo's interest in scale disjunctions and layered spaces combined with an effusive love of pop culture.

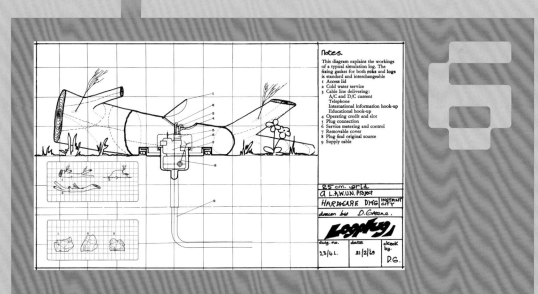

David Greene, Logplug, 1969

Radical contextualism. David Greene's Logplug and Rokplug are about both the dissolution of architecture under the influence of new electronic forms of communication and the ultimate piece of Post-Modern contextualisation. The miserable constraint of 'fitting in' here becomes a subversive act of cultural camouflage, the Trojan Horse of technology hidden behind a Beatrix Potter pastoralism.

7

Hans Hollein, Aircraft Carrier City in Landscape, 1964

Radical decontextualism. Hollein's drawing uses collage to create a violent displacement of object and field, form and content. This is the opposite of commercial Post-Modernism's desire to 'fit in' or politely obey urban design rules, a latent strand of Post-Modernism that is more concerned with radical disjunction, difference and juxtaposition.

Dan Graham, Alteration to a Suburban House, 1978

This project is radically Post-Modern in the first place through its simultaneous juxtaposition of two distinct 20th-century spatialities – the transparencies of Miesian space and the repetitive conformity of Levittown-inspired suburbia. By removing the front wall of the tract house and replacing it with a piece of plate glass, the private life of the American nuclear family – normally abruptly segregated from the life of the street – is exposed to the public realm.

By bisecting the house longitudinally with a mirror wall, the living spaces are not only exposed to the outside but the inhabitants are made even more self-conscious as their previously private actions are exposed to both the outside world and themselves. The mirror also brings the previously segregated exterior world of the neighbourhood emphatically into the interior. However, the new window on the interior and the opportunities it presents to the external viewer are undermined by the ability of voyeurs to see themselves in the mirror, making them self-consciously aware of their own voyeurism. In setting up these relationships, Graham charges the abstract space of Modernism with pyschological meaning, in a way that reinforces and contradicts the territories of privacy, security and voyeurism within suburban space. It is this charging of the space to create resonances beyond the claimed neutrality of Modernist spaces that makes this a radically Post-Modern project.

Richard Hamilton, *Just what is it that makes today's homes so different, so appealing?*, 1956

Arguably the first work of Pop Art, this collage could also claim to be the first Post-Modern architectural space. It is a highly sophisticated, skewed space of the type that was to become characteristic of works by Moore, Isozaki and Hollein. Equally radically, it is a space that is charged by its contents, which comprise consumer durables culled from advertising images, human beings whose very corporeality is mediated and commodified, and a world beyond that shows what Marshall McLuhan described as the extensions of that corporeality – the new 'electric' technologies of moving image and sound. In other words it describes the 'space' of the later 20th and early 21st century more eloquently and realistically than any architectural drawing has managed since. It constitutes a radical architectural space, as it is constructed not through drawings, as architecture always was at that point, but by collage, using as-found elements already carrying their own significations and constructing a semiological space enabling these significations to interact. This represented a spatial understanding far in advance of that predominating in architecture which, at the time, generally thought of space as a neutral geometric entity.

9

OMA, Parc de la Villette, Paris, 1982

10

The park is laid out as a series of programmed strips running north to south. Over these are laid various paths, routes, kiosks, buildings and existing structures. However, the radical move is the setting up of wildly disparate and therefore unstable programmatic adjacencies in relation to each other – a horizontal manifestation of Rem Koolhaas' 'Culture of Congestion' as emblematicised in the section of New York's Downtown Athletic Club (1930) with its vertical stacking of programmes. The plan of La Villette overlaid the strip fields of the Dutch polder into the interstitial space between historic Paris and its *banlieue* beyond the *periferique*, which bordered the site to the north. This configuration of geometric space formed a framework designed to contain the excesses of metropolitan life and to acknowledge its instability, in the same way that the Manhattan skyscraper's programme remains ever changing and yet contained within a powerful urban form. The strip plan combines all kinds of programmes ranging from sports to fake deserts and from agriculture to hedonistic playground. Each strip can be experienced individually as a singular experience (albeit inflected by the programmes either side) or, by traversing all of the strips, as a multiplicity of glimpses across a series of turbulent programmatic experiences. Again, this constitutes the opposite of neutral, geometric Modernist space. It is a space of contradictions, contaminations and congestions, a space charged with programmatic hedonism. ⚙

COUNTERPOINT

Jayne Merkel

NOT SO RADICAL AN AMERICAN PERSPECTIVE

Jayne Merkel relishes the opportunity to talk about architecture in the light of communication, context, wider culture, 'the ordinary', new technology and aesthetic affect – all topics that are back on the agenda with this issue on Radical Post-Modernism. However, she provides a view from Manhattan that calls into question the possible re-emergence of a 'Radical Post-Modern' movement in North America, although some members of the American architectural establishment continue to practice PoMo even if they do not preach it.

FAT's lively revival of Post-Modern moves may seem 'radical' at a time when convoluted abstract architectural form is the style *du jour* and Post-Modernism is rarely mentioned. So this issue is a welcome addition to the current scene. A reconsideration of ideas that began to surface among prominent American Modern architects in the 1950s and that were developed in Robert Venturi's 1966 *Complexity and Contradiction in Architecture*[1] is long overdue. And it is great fun to have Charles Jencks, who popularised Venturi's programme and other notions in the air at the time, championing the development once again. It is time to talk about communication in architecture, the value of context, the culture beyond architecture, the

importance of the ordinary, the real potential of technology and ways to use minimal means for aesthetic effect.

Despite a lack of conversation on the subject, on this side of the Atlantic it is not unusual, and certainly not radical, to *do* Post-Modernism. It just seems to be taboo to *talk* about it. Three of the four most prominent original practitioners of the style (Robert Venturi, Michael Graves and Robert AM Stern) are still working within some version of it (the fourth, Charles Moore, died in 1993). And, for a variety of reasons, some younger American architects are using some of the flat (or almost flat) decorative elements and communicative devices that the FAT partners celebrate here. They are mining historic and vernacular sources and engaging the general public cleverly. They are even sometimes self-consciously using architecture to make the world a better place. This does not, however, add up to the arrival of a new age of Radical Post-Modernism, and certainly not to one that appeared with the drop of the Centennial New Year's ball abruptly in 2000.

Modern architecture was always more a style than a movement in the US. It arrived, not in Bauhaus workshops intended to use technology to house the masses decently, but at the Museum of Modern Art (MoMA) in a travelling show curated by Henry Russell Hitchcock, Philip Johnson, Lewis Mumford and Alfred Barr. Although it was called 'Modern Architects', had a section on housing and contained work by several American architects (including Frank Lloyd Wright), it is often confused with a book Hitchcock and Johnson published the same year, which concentrated on European work, emphasised aesthetics and was called *The International Style*.[2]

Because of the Great Depression and the Second World War, International Style Modern architecture did not make an impact on American streets until the late 1940s. And by the mid-1950s many of the most prominent American Modern architects (Philip Johnson, Eero Saarinen, Louis Kahn, Paul Rudolph, John Johansen and Edward

Durell Stone) were already growing restless.
All but Stone were featured in a 1961 issue
of the Yale Architecture Journal *Perspecta 7*[3]
where they admitted an interest in imagery
and the past. Still, despite bold references
to historic forms in Johnson's Guest House
renovation of 1953, Stone's US Embassy in
New Delhi of 1954–9, Saarinen's Morse and
Stiles Colleges at Yale of 1958–62 (which
provoked Reyner Banham to write 'Yale is
a very sick place'), it was not until Venturi's
Complexity appeared, five years later, that the
seeds were sewn for a movement.

Although Venturi never called himself a
Post-Modernist (the current proscription goes
way back), the work he did – and does – fits
the definition. He made a well-reasoned case
for the importance of history, symbolism and
decoration. Soon all these things entered
the mainstream of architectural practice in
the US, but made a much greater impact
on the East Coast and in places where Ivy
League architecture schools (particularly
Yale, Princeton and Penn) had influence.
Not only young architects (like Graves and
Stern) embraced the style. Some good older
Modernists (such as Bruce Graham and Kevin
Roche) came under its influence, often with
rather disastrous results, and big commercial
firms started placing decorative crowns on
their skyscrapers and colonnades around their
bases. Soon overexposure led to boredom, and
the style went out of style. But the most original
practitioners kept doing it – and still do.

Venturi, who now practises with his
wife, Denise Scott Brown, as Venturi, Scott
Brown and Associates (VSBA), continues
to cover his facades with flat decoration
connoting the purpose of the building
or referring to something nearby. Graves
still works with the very personal stylised
classical language he developed decades
ago, applying it not only to buildings of
many kinds all over the world, but to
everything inside as well, to household
wares sold both at high-design shops and
at the Target 'big box' budget stores. Stern
has abandoned the clever simplified original
references to historical styles of his youth for
a more direct contextualism.

'I was an enthusiast for ironic quotation,'
he explains. 'I used that as a strategy to
figure my way of the kind of Modernism
I had been impregnated with through my
education. Then I began to see that the joke
can only last for a short time. Architecture
is a serious business, by and large, and I
began to investigate more and more seriously
the historic languages that had always been
what architects knew. And then I began to
think of myself as a modern traditionalist,
sometimes a modern vernacularist,
sometimes a modern classicist. Because
one of the great important lessons of Post-
Modernism is the building in its context.[4]

Stern's early work is more original, but his
recent buildings attract a large appreciative
audience. His firm receives commissions
from numerous prestigious universities, and
his very traditional condominiums in New
York City outsell those by stars like Herzog
& de Meuron, Jean Nouvel and Frank Gehry,
and other architects whom students admire
today. Stern's 'prewar style' apartments at 15
Central Park West command higher prices
than any in the city, except the traditional
ones carved out of the old Plaza Hotel, which
is equally popular with the overly affluent.

In 1998, when Stern was named Dean
of the Yale School of Architecture, people

Alexander Gorlin Architects, Nehemiah Spring Creek, Brooklyn, New York, 2008
below: Gorlin's subsidised row houses for low-income residents recall historic ones while frankly and festively displaying their prefabricated construction.

Architecture Research Office (ARO), Armed Forces Recruiting Station, Times Square, New York, 1999
bottom and opposite left: This building as sign – or as symbol – transforms a simple functional structure into an icon, blending into the lively street scene while transforming a simple little government building into something both contextual and exciting.

WXY Architects, Times Square pavement redesign, 2010
opposite right: The lively reflective pattern of the pavement emphasises the transformation of this central tourist area into a pedestrian space instead of a congested, traffic-clogged corridor.

Although the early Modernist ambition to use architecture to improve social conditions was lost as artistic freedom was gained, some of the most interesting public and philanthropic work being done in New York has PoMo undertones.

worried that it would turn into a hotbed of Post-Modernism, which was then, as a style, way out of style. But as dean he has emphasised the eclectic (as opposed to the stylistic) aspect of Post-Modernism, and brought in people with as wide a range of points of view as possible – from Zaha Hadid to FAT. Next year, Agents of Change will teach there. The Post-Modern concern for the context lives on, mandated by law in many parts of the US. Most of the 27,000 buildings protected by New York City's 1965 Landmarks Law are parts of historic districts. Only 1,265 buildings have individual landmark status.

And even though many architects – and most commercial firms – stopped using overt references to historic buildings by the middle of the 1980s, the Modernist proscription against art for art's sake, decoration for decoration's sake, the insistence on rigorous truth to materials and minimal means of expression never regained fully fledged favour. Post-Modernism simply made more things possible, as the wide array of ways of working by the various practices that FAT applaud here shows.

Although the early Modernist ambition to use architecture to improve social conditions was lost as artistic freedom was gained, some of the most interesting public and philanthropic work being done in New York has PoMo undertones. This trend represents something of a departure, since

in America the old Post-Modernism and community-based architecture were usually on different trajectories. Alexander Gorlin, a mid-career architect who designed unusually beautiful, sophisticated Post-Modern houses in his youth and then adopted a simplified Modernist vocabulary for the mansions and institutional buildings he usually does, has designed the largest group of subsidised row houses ever proposed in New York. The first 117 of the 800 low-cost row houses at Nehemiah Spring Creek, which were developed by a coalition of churches on an 18-hectare (45-acre) former landfill site in East Brooklyn were completed three years ago. Gorlin's prefabricated houses recall traditional New York row houses in a frank, crisp modern way that made it possible to offer 149-square-metre (1,600-square-foot) units for as little as $158,000.

Almost every architect who has built in Times Square during the last few decades has responded very directly to

**WXY Architects, Sea Glass Carousel,
Battery Park, New York, 2011**
below: Daytime view teasingly suggesting
the aquarium-like atmosphere of the 21st-
century electronic carousel.

bottom: At night the brightly lit electronic
carousel becomes both a beacon and a
symbol of the history of the area within
which it is located.

At the southern tip of Manhattan in Battery Park, the first
part of the island to be settled and the first location of the city's
Aquarium, WXY is building a glowing High Tech carousel
with floating fishes to recall the original residents of the area.

FreeGreen Architecture, Traditional House Design, New Orleans, Louisiana, 2010
left: This rather conventional design with a gabled roof and prominent front porch won the US Green Building Council Natural Talent Design Competition for an LEED platinum affordable home last year.

FreeGreen Architecture, The Suburban Loft, 2010
right: Model of a sustainable house that can be purchased online and built anywhere in the US. The most popular of the numerous styles of affordable zero-energy houses sold on the Internet by FreeGreen is surprisingly modern.

the lively context, but probably the most daring building is, of all things, an armed forces recruiting station, designed by the Architectural Research Office (ARO) in 1999. Stephen Cassells and Adam Yarinksy of ARO covered the walls of the one-room, boxy, glass-walled structure with fluorescent tubes that create an American flag, a design that acquired additional meaning after 9/11. Nearby, WXY (formerly Weisz + Yoes) Architecture is using a shiny egg-shaped pattern on the pavement of the streets in Times Square, most of which have been returned to pedestrian use. These mid-career architects like working in the public realm.

At the southern tip of Manhattan in Battery Park, the first part of the island to be settled and the first location of the city's aquarium, WXY is building a glowing High Tech carousel with floating fishes to recall the original residents of the area. It is another by-product of Post-Modernism with its symbolism, figuration and wit, as well as a product of recent electronic technology.

These projects are exciting and delightful but they are not really 'radical', nor are the practices that created them and the ones celebrated in this issue. A radical practice is FreeGreen, a firm in Boston, that provides free plans for green houses in a variety of styles on a website supported by advertising. Ben Uyeda, the chief architectural officer, and his partners, who studied engineering and business, met at Cornell. They were all interested in sustainability, and thought they could do something about it together.

Since 49 per cent of all energy is used by buildings, and houses are the most common building type, they started a company, Zero Energy Design, in 2006, to create unusually efficient homes. But they soon realised that since houses are so labour intensive, it only pays to design expensive ones and therefore they could only effect a tiny percentage of the market. However, by selling plans and details for green houses on a website supported by advertising, they could make a really significant difference. As the FreeGreen website notes: 'With 98,774 house plans downloaded (and counting), FreeGreen is the world's largest provider of home design' – and it was inspired by environmentalism. They also found that though conventional wisdom holds that few American home-

**Michael Graves Architects, Resorts World
Sentosa, Singapore, 2010**
The architects won this $4.32 billion
commission for a 50-hectare (121-acre)
glamorous and 'green' resort with six
hotels, restaurants, underground casinos,
a 1,600-seat theatre, marina, spa,
museums, and play areas in a 2006
international developer's competition.

buyers are interested in modern design, their most popular model is the clearly modern Suburban Loft.

Up to this point, computer technology has mainly been used to design and construct new kinds of buildings and the Internet to disseminate information about them, emphasising form and making instantaneous archi-stars. FreeGreen's use of the Web takes architecture in a whole new direction, but one offering all kinds of styles, in tune with the Post-Modern project. But their interest is in sustainability. An open-minded attitude towards style is merely a means to an end.

The American architects who do work that has Post-Modern qualities do not tend to talk or think about things in terms of styles. Young architects and students follow individual architects (such as Gehry, Hadid and Herzog & de Meuron), but not really movements, though parametricism is occasionally mentioned.

Still, the editors of this issue of ⌀ may be on to something. The recent Thirtieth

Anniversary issue of *Metropolis* magazine contains a series of essays on various movements of the last three decades, accompanied by a Jencksian chart that lists and summarises them. However, the first essay, which is on PoMo, by Mark Lamster begins: 'A friend asks, "So what are you working on?" I respond, "An essay on postmodernism." Now recoiling with a look of horrified bafflement, he says, "Good lord, why?" I have had this exchange any number of times since I took this assignment.'[5]

Clearly, Post-Modernism has not yet arrived on these shores with a bang. ⌀

Notes
1. Robert Venturi, *Complexity and Contradiction in Architecture*, The Museum of Modern Art (New York) in association with the Graham Foundation for Advanced Studies in The Fine Arts (Chicago), 1966.
2. One reason for the confusion is that Terrence Riley organised an exhibition at Columbia University entitled 'The International Style: Exhibition 15 and The Museum of Modern Art', which was accompanied by a catalogue in which Philip Johnson wrote in the foreword: 'It is just 60 years since the exhibition, "Modern Architecture," was opened at The Museum of Modern Art,' p 5. The

catalogue was published by Rizzoli with Columbia Books on Architecture as Catalogue 3 (both in New York) in 1992. The title of the catalogue of the original exhibition, however, was *Modern Architects*, Museum of Modern Art and WW Norton & Company (New York), 1932. The book by Henry Russell Hitchcock and Philip Johnson of the same year was titled *The International Style: Architecture Since 1922*, WW Norton & Company (New York), 1932.
3. Lawrence Cox (ed), *Perspecta 7*, Yale Architectural Journal (New Haven, CT), 1961; the issue contained articles by or interviews with Philip Johnson, Eero Saarinen, Paul Rudolph, Louis Kahn, John Johansen and articles by Sybil Moholy-Nagy ('The Future of the Past', pp 65–76,), James Gowan ('Notes on American Architecture', pp 77–82), Walter McQuade ('The Exploded Landscape', pp 83–90), Peter Collins ('The Form-Givers', pp 91–6) and Colin St John Wilson ('Open and Closed', 97–102).
4. Recorded telephone interview with Robert AM Stern, 8 April 2011.
5. 'Post-Modernism, pomo returns (or maybe it never left)', *Metropolis Special Anniversary Issue: 1981–2011*, April 2011, p 68. The Jencksian chart appears on pp 66–7.

Eva Branscome is a PhD candidate at the Bartlett School of Architecture, University College London (UCL). She is currently investigating architectural Post-Modernism and how the postwar art scene in Vienna can inform this debate. Prior to this she has worked as an expert on Modern architecture for the pressure group the Twentieth Century Society, lobbying for the retention of the best buildings of that era. Most recently she has collaborated on the new edition of Charles Jencks' *The Post-Modern Reader* (Wiley, 2011).

Jayne Merkel is a New York-based architectural historian and critic, and a contributing editor of both ᗜ in London and *Architectural Record* in New York. She is the author of *Eero Saarinen* (Phaidon Press, 2005) and an Emmy-award-winning scriptwriter of the documentary film *The Gateway Arch, A Reflection of America* (2006). A former editor of *Oculus* magazine in New York and architecture critic of *The Cincinnati Enquirer*, her writing has appeared in *Architecture, Art in America, Artforum, Connoisseur, Design Book Review, Harvard Design Magazine* and the *Wilson Quarterly*. She directed the Graduate Program in Architecture and Design Criticism at Parsons School of Design in New York, taught writing at the University of Cincinnati and art history at the Rhode Island School of Design, Miami University in Ohio and the Art Academy of Cincinnati.

Kester Rattenbury is an architectural writer and teacher. She trained as an architect and completed a PhD on the coverage of architecture in the UK national press, which resulted in her first book, *This Is Not Architecture: Media Constructions* (Routledge, 2002). She has published many books, has worked as an architectural journalist both nationally and internationally, and teaches at the University of Westminster where she is Reader in Architecture and runs the research group EXP, whose projects include the Supercrit series and the Archigram Archival Project. Her most recent research is an exploration of the role of architecture in classic English novels.

Léa-Catherine Szacka studied architecture in Canada and Italy before entering the PhD programme at the Bartlett School of Architecture, UCL, with her thesis on 'Exhibiting the Post-Modern: Three Narratives for a History of the 1980 Venice Architecture Biennale'. In 2010 she was a scholar of the British School at Rome and taught architecture at Nottingham Trent University. She has also worked for the Barbican Art Centre in London, the Centre Pompidou in Paris and Actar publishers in Barcelona, while collaborating with various newspapers and magazines. Most recently she collaborated on the new edition of Charles Jencks' *The Post-Modern Reader* (Wiley, 2011)

INDIVIDUAL BACKLIST ISSUES OF △D ARE
AVAILABLE FOR PURCHASE AT £22.99 / US$45
TO ORDER AND SUBSCRIBE SEE BELOW

What is Architectural Design?

Founded in 1930, *Architectural Design* (△D) is an influential and prestigious publication. It combines the currency and topicality of a newsstand journal with the rigour and production qualities of a book. With an almost unrivalled reputation worldwide, it is consistently at the forefront of cultural thought and design.

Each title of △D is edited by an invited guest-editor, who is an international expert in the field. Renowned for being at the leading edge of design and new technologies, △D also covers themes as diverse as: architectural history, the environment, interior design, landscape architecture and urban design.

Provocative and inspirational, △D inspires theoretical, creative and technological advances. It questions the outcome of technical innovations as well as the far-reaching social, cultural and environmental challenges that present themselves today.

For further information on △D, subscriptions and purchasing single issues see: www.architectural-design-magazine.com

How to Subscribe

With 6 issues a year, you can subscribe to △D (either print or online), or buy titles individually.

Subscribe today to receive 6 issues delivered direct to your door!

INSTITUTIONAL SUBSCRIPTION
£230 / US$431 combined print & online

INSTITUTIONAL SUBSCRIPTION
£200 / US$375 print or online

INDIVIDUAL RATE SUBSCRIPTION
£120 / US$189 print only

STUDENT RATE SUBSCRIPTION
£75 / US$117 print only

To subscribe:
Tel: +44 (0) 1243 843272
Email: cs-journals@wiley.com

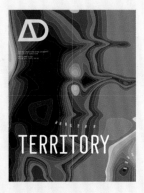

Volume 80 No 3
ISBN 978 0470 721650

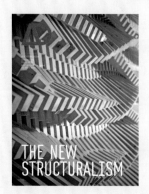

Volume 80 No 4
ISBN 978 0470 742273

Volume 80 No 5
ISBN 978 0470 744987

Volume 80 No 6
ISBN 978 0470 746622

Volume 81 No 1
ISBN 978 0470 747209

Volume 81 No 2
ISBN 978 0470 748282

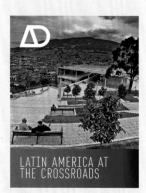

Volume 81 No 3
ISBN 978 0470 664926

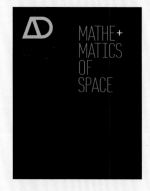

Volume 81 No 4
ISBN 978 0470 689806